# WOMEN FACING LOSS:

# DISEASE, BEREAVEMENT, AND EMOTIONAL RESPONSE

Margot Tallmer, Florence Selder, Austin H. Kutscher,
Mary-Ellen Siegel and Elizabeth B. Clark,
Editors

Roberta Halporn, Executive Editor

DEDICATED TO THE MEMORY OF
THERESA HERBERT

Copyright © 1996 by the Foundation of Thanatology
New York, N.Y.

ISSN 0193-6379

ISBN 0-930194-40-3

Production Office

Foundation Book and Periodical Division
c/o The Center
391 Atlantic Avenue
Brooklyn, N.Y. 11217-1701

# EDITORIAL BOARD

Arthur S. Berger, J.D.
Sandra L. Bertman, E.D.M.
Peter D. Birkett, M.D
Martin H. Blitzer, D.D.S
Daniel J. Cherico, Ph.D, M.P.H.
Elizabeth J. Clark, Ph.D., A.C.S.W.
Janice I. Cohn, D.S.W.
L. Jeannette Davis, C.S.W.
Kenneth J. Doka, Ph.D.
Frances K. Forstenzer, L.C.S.W.
Jerome L. Fredrick, Ph.D.
Carolyn L. Garson, R.N., M.S.
Margaret J. Grey, D.P.H.
Roberta Halporn, M.A.
Frederick C. Hartman, Ph.D.
Sherry E. Johnson, R.N., Ph.D.
Joan M. Kaiser, R.N., M.A.
Elizabeth Krajic Kachur, Ph.D.

Austin H. Kutscher
Carole A. Lambert
Charles W. Lochner, M.S., M.A.
Mary Dee McEvoy, M.S., R.N.
Thomas McGovern, Ed.D.
Hilda N. Quiles, R.D.H.
Patricia M. Reddish, M.S., N.C.S.
Joel Savishinsky, Ph.D.
Arlene Seguine, Ed.D.
Florence E. Selder, R.N., Ph.D.
Virginia Sendor, M.S., M.P.A.
Donald L. Sherak, M.D.
Robert G. Stevenson, Ed.D.
Ursula Thunberg, M.D.
Adrian R. Tiemann, Ph.D
William Weiner, A.C.S.W.
Susan K. Westlake
David Wollner, M.D.

# CONTENTS

## I. Societal Influences on Women's Losses

1. Women and Loss: Dealing with Uncertainty .............. 1
    Florence E. Selder

2. Woman, Body, and Self Image ....................... 11
    Irene B. Seeland

3. Love Shock. The Phenomena Involved in the Management of Individuals Facing the Loss of a Love Relationship .......... 17
    Stephen V. Gullo and Henry Berger

4. Social Aspects of Sexual Loss: A Radical Essay ................................ 25
    David Wendell Moeller

5. The Changing Place of Women in the Professions ..................................... 33
    Meta Goswami

## II. Disease, Treatment, and Loss

6. The Meaning of Death and Loss for Women .............. 41
    Don Sloan

7. The Effects of Radiation Therapy and Gynecologic Cancers ................................ 45
    Richard Torpie

8. Utilizing Health Information after the Diagnoses of Breast Cancer: A Health Education Program Model ......... 49
    Rose M. Savage Jackman

9. Coping With AIDS in an Inner City Population ............ 61
    Chantal Bruchez-Hall, Nanette Nelson, and Anita Sussman

8. The Nurse and Acute Death: Dealing with the Threat of Death in the Cardiac Surgery Unit ..................... 71
   Richard S. Blacher and Margaret M. Bedard

## III. Infertility and Pregnancy Loss

9. The Grief of Miscarriage ............................... 75
   Dorothy M. Hai and Mark S. Tong

10. Staff Reactions to Fetal Demise ........................ 85
    Yvonne M. Parnes

11. Grieving Without God ................................. 89
    Marion Cohen

12. Patients' Dissatisfaction with Medical Care: The Case of Pregnancy Loss ..................................... 93
    Judith Lasker

## IV. Life Cycle Losses

13. Anticipatory Grief of the Urban Single Mother For her Male Child ................................... 103
    Lavone Hazell

14. The Myth of the Empty Nest Syndrome ................. 107
    Margot Tallmer

15. Widows Who Participated in a Red Cross Widow's Program ... 113
    Dorothea R. Hays

16. A Pastoral View of Widowhood ........................ 123
    Carole Smith-Torres

17. Suicide in the Elderly ................................. 125
    Margot Tallmer

    Contributors ......................................... 136

# WOMEN AND LOSS: DEALING WITH UNCERTAINTY

## Florence Selder

*Introduction*

A useful framework for understanding women's responses to real or perceived losses is the life transition theory. The life transition theory describes how people restructure their realities after a disrupting event. If the disrupting event lies initially outside the awareness of the individual or is external to the individual, then the event is called a critical incident, whereas if the individual is aware, at some level, of a choice regarding the event, then it is described as a determined decision.[1] In either case, the event must be sufficiently disruptive that a reorganization of the existing reality and the construction of a new one are necessitated.

Women encounter losses of various types throughout their lives. What determines a loss as a disrupting event is personal and self-defined, and entails relinquishing of a relationship with oneself, another person, or an object, or letting go of an experience within one's reality system. The disruption is such that it requires the woman to acknowledge that she must give up some significant aspect of her reality. Certain assumptions exist in anyone's reality system at any one time, and when one of these becomes absent or threatens to become absent, then the reality, as it is, cannot be maintained. Then reality must be redesigned, reconstructed, re-evaluated, or reconceptualized in such a way that the disrupting event is no longer central to one's life. The ultimate reality to be structured will be determined by the woman's expectations, and she will structure her experiences in such a way as to find meaning in them.

Inherent in the potential realities that could be constructed is the issue of one's sense of self, or identity-constancy. Throughout the transition, the focus is the realignment of oneself and the regaining of one's intactness/integrity following the disruption. In cases when a woman does not acknowledge the changed aspect in her reality, her engagement in active living or creating is absent or greatly curtailed. Consider the type of woman who for ten years grieves for her dead husband, and simultaneously acts as if he were alive. This woman continues to define her reality as a wife, and fails to construct a new reality in which the dead husband is no longer the focus of her life.[2]

A definitive passage of temporality is required for the restructuring of a person's reality. For instance, with the simple passage of time, that which was lost or perceived as lost usually becomes less central to one's life. The process of diminishing the primacy of the loss operates through an integration of the loss experience. This may be accomplished by finding some meaning in the loss, or through a releasing of the loss experience (i.e., absence of meaning in the loss), or by encapsulating the loss (e.g., not engaging either in meaning or no meaning). A life transition bridges the pre-loss reality with the newly constructed or emerged reality. The duration of the life transition lasts from the initial awareness of the experience of loss, to the perception of the loss as not occupying primary space in one's life. For individual women, the factor that initiates the life transition is highly selective and self defined.[3]

*Uncertainty*

The major characteristic of the life transition following a loss is uncertainty. The sources of uncertainty are related to temporal factors, personal factors, and the nature of the loss. Temporal factors contribute to the uncertainty in the life transition by changes in perceptions of time. Prior to a loss, a woman may operate on what is frequently described as linear time, which is the organization of events by time: e.g., there are twenty-four hours in one day and that each portion of each day is allocated to certain activities. A person marks the location of events by clock time designation. Mealtime is identified by certain hour parameters. Clock time is also described as linear or closed system time.

Following a loss, it is suggested that a person organizes time by events. Events, and not clock time, become the chronological landmarks which structure the emerging reality post-loss. For instance, women report "losing track of time," in the form of calendar or clock time (e.g., days, weeks, hours) and report that they designate time by signifying events: e.g. "the day I cleaned out John's closet," or, "the day I gave away his suits." As the woman relates to others who are not dealing with a disrupted reality, she experiences a subjective confusion and a reported sense of not being oriented to time, person or place. The woman is indeed oriented to time, person and place, but within a different temporal structure. However, she reports being disturbed by the change in time structuring, and reports feeling uncertain. The confusion exists because she has no sense of time and space shared with someone not in the transition. Associates and friends who are not in the transition generally operate on a linear time structure, while the woman in the transition functions within non-linear time. Non-linear time is useful for the transitional person, as it provides an efficient means of responding to the loss; the event has primacy, not the time-context. A change in time-structuring also results in failure to project into the future. Any future projection is greatly curtailed in the life transition, because a future orientation entails a linear perspective which encompasses past, present and future, and is embedded in a time context, whereas an event context is characterized by pending shifts in reality and outside clock time.

To illustrate, a woman will report being unable to imagine not being with the child who died, not being married, or not living with her lover. For her, time is compressed or collapsed. Following the loss, a woman appears to be preoccupied with the reality that preceded the loss. For example, during divorce proceedings, a woman may repeatedly review the marriage relationship. Some clinicians describe the review as obsessive.

The preoccupation of the recent and pre-loss reality is a requisite condition of the life transition. Women whose infants died soon after birth report an incessant review of the nine months preceding the child's birth/death and an obsessive review of the infant's first few minutes/hours/days/months of life. Understandably, one is more attuned to the recent pre-loss reality, in which there is less uncertainty, than in the unconstructed and unstructured reality which is out of the immediate awareness of the woman: e.g., the reality of not having a living child. The engagement in the pre-loss reality functions to enable the woman to become aware of her position of known and changed circumstances. This process provides a means of structuring a new reality. To begin to structure a new reality, one must become aware that the previous reality lacks utility and is no longer functional.

The personal factors that contribute to uncertainty are those that require a woman to structure a reality that is consistent with her previous sense of self. After a loss, women will report not knowing who they are, and being unsure of who they will become. For example, the woman whose marriage or relationship is terminated by a divorce/separation/death will experience a loss in terms of the uncoupling of a dyad. Her pattern of relating to the world as part of a paired couple is disrupted. If a relationship has been important to one's sense of self, then the custom of caring for, and being responsible to and for someone, contributes to the uncertainty once the focus is changed. The experience of uncertainty stems from the disruption of a socially-sanctioned and publicly recognized role which has contributed to one's self-definition. The meaning and belonging that one derived from the coupled state now demands re-evaluation.

Each woman has a sense of self which is described as identity constancy: the stable condition of being oneself. A disrupting event impacts on the person's identity constancy. For example, prior to the decision to lose weight, a woman derives some notion of her body boundaries in terms of her clothing size. After a weight loss of more than fifty pounds, a woman may consistently gravitate to the clothing size that she wore prior to the weight loss. Her identity constancy has not been realigned to conform to the new reality of being thin. To maintain thinness, a woman must establish an identity constancy that is congruent with the new reality.

Last, the nature of the loss contributes to uncertainty. The nature of the loss (e.g. death, separation) is unique, both to the context of the event and to the person experiencing the loss. The meaning of the loss can only be defined by the person who experiences it. Some commonly shared experiences exist within each loss, and these form the basis for the success of support groups. However a part of the disrupted reality is always unshareable, and it must be experienced singularly by the woman, as she attempts to create or restructure a reality that integrates, encapsulates or disengages the loss event.

In an attempt to decrease uncertainty, the woman will seek information around the loss event. The seeking of information may be about the context of the loss: e.g., the facts of the child's death, or the reasons for one's husband leaving.

Two other factors, relative to the nature of the loss, contribute to uncertainty. First, knowledge about women's responses to losses is limited. Such lack of information compounds the ambiguity and uncertainty. No "map" is available for maneuvering through the transition following loss, and the woman thus remains uncertain which of her responses might facilitate closure to the transition. Secondly, following the loss, the woman frequently reports inability to remember information, and to interpret the intentions of others toward her. Information that is not grasped or that is distorted fails to provide the woman with the means to understand her situation, and contributes to the uncertainty she is experiencing.

*Structuring for Awareness*

To reiterate, a disrupting event that brings about a loss to a woman will bring about permanent changes in her reality.[4] From her initial awareness, the woman must come to terms with the permanency of the loss. She must either acknowledge or not acknowledge awareness of the loss. A major achievement in this situation, which supports engagement in the life transition, is ability to acknowledge the irreversibility of the loss. This acknowledgment permits the woman to engage in the transition. Conditional acknowledgment is the admission of a fact, attenuated by a modifying circumstance, which enables the woman to acknowledge the loss while maintaining some qualifications. For example, women responding to a disability/chronic illness frequently report conditional acknowledgment: e.g., "There's always a miracle."

Non-acknowledgment is failure to acknowledge the loss or its consequences or the resultant changed circumstances. It is essential that the woman acknowledge its irreversibility, and begin to relinquish the pre-loss reality. Refusing to acknowledge the permanency of the changed reality results in a failure to structure a new reality. For example, some women who are no longer wives still function and perceive themselves as wives; they view the ex-husband's new wife as the non-wife (e.g., "other woman") and wait for the day that the ex-husband will return.

Once the woman acknowledges the loss, she must still become aware of the consequences of the loss, and their impact on her life. It must be remembered that a loss implies profound changes, and she must learn to incorporate and manage them. The process of making changes that are supportive of the woman's expectations and self perception is inherent in the life transition. The process of the life transition is dynamic, and requires some deliberation on her part. In short, she must become aware of the loss, of the consequences and of possible options. The concepts of 1) missed options, 2) trigger events, and 3) time in the transition function to facilitate awareness. The purpose of structuring for awareness processes is to move the person from a position of changed circumstances that are unrecognized, to an ability to start becoming able to redefine the circumstances. The intrinsic function of the process is to make the person aware, and to create meaning in her changed circumstances, and thus construct a new reality.

Trigger events are occurrences which precipitate awareness of the dysfunctional or useless reality,[5] and bring about recognition of the implications of change. The trigger events include reactivation and irrevocability.

Reactivation is the awareness of thoughts, feelings and sensations reminiscent of those that occurred prior to, or early in, the life transition. For example, a woman who hears noises in the upstairs bedroom momentarily thinks, "Oh, John is getting up", only to immediately recall that John is dead. Initially, the tears and the immediate feelings of loneliness are as intense as the first experience of the loss. With recurrent reactivation, the woman's responses will become less intense. It is essential that women know about reactivation, and view it as a sign of progress rather than as a sign that they have not resolved their grief conflict. Reactivation is also very frightening; therefore, an understanding of it, and of its utility, helps to decrease the anxiety it evokes.

Another trigger event is irrevocability. Irrevocability is the awareness of the irreversibility or permanency of a changed reality. The task of sorting a lost spouse's clothes and personal belongings brings about an awareness of the permanency of the event. Women report that this chore marks an important turning point for them. At the other extreme, a woman recently seen by the author had never performed the task of sorting her spouse's personal belongings although her husband has been dead for ten years. As the woman sorts the personal belonging of the dead spouse and decides on their disposal, she becomes aware of the permanency of the changed reality; in not sorting the possessions, she is slowing or curtailing such awareness. Allocating the spouse's possessions or filing for divorce, are tasks frequently delayed because they force such an awareness.

Besides the two trigger events identified, another means of structuring for awareness is by identifying missed options: that is, the delimiting of the behaviors or experiences which a person previously claimed as part of his or her reality. Identifying missed options is an important part of responding to a loss, as it provides a means of facilitating the transition from the pre-loss reality to the structuring of a new one. Very clearly, the death of one's infant is a missed option, and it means that one will not be a mother, one will never parent that particular child, one will not watch the child become an adult, and one will not have the once-expected bond with the infant that the prior nine months had promised as a possibility.

In a less dramatic way, a missed option is reported by one woman who said that whenever she was out of town and awakened in the middle of the night, she would call her live-in friend. His response was always, "Oh hi, how are you, what time is it, ...okay.....glad you called!" She always felt comforted and cared for. After the relationship ended, she realized that making a phone call in the middle of the night was no longer an option for her. She reported missing that option much more than she missed the man.

Missed options frequently symbolize the meaning of the relationship with the lost object. These are the aspects of the relationship that are sorely missed. They are unique to the individual and an outside observer might too easily minimize them. Beware of doing so! The identification of missed options is a means of achieving awareness of the inaccessibility of the pre-loss reality. Therefore, it is not surprising that the missed options identified comprise the significant attachments felt by the client in his/her relationship to the previous reality. If missed options are not acknowledged, then the person remains in the pre-loss reality.

The function of the processes, e.g., trigger events and missed options in structuring for awareness, is to enable the woman to begin to create a new reality. One must become aware that there is loss, and that this discontinuation is irreversible. One cannot continue in a reality that no longer exists. Thus an important task is to recognize the permanency of the changes. The time in the transition, reduces uncertainty about the woman's disrupted life. The doubts, the "what-ifs" and the magical thinking of what was lost being returned, begins to be diminished by the awareness-structuring processes.

Once permanency is acknowledged, uncertainty is initially reduced. Once the person actually acknowledges even in a conditional manner that the loved one will not return; that functional ability reduced by a disease/disability will not be restored; that one's life is changed, the uncertainty decreases.

At this time, the quest for additional information is reduced; the person no longer seeks information about the reasons for the spouse's death, about how the lover/spouse is doing, about absolute cures for an illness/disability, about what went wrong with a pregnancy; or about the events surrounding the death of a child. A change occurs from seeking information to realizing that information retrieval is no longer useful. Knowing more does not reduce uncertainty.

Information initially reduces uncertainty because it helps the woman explain or understand what has happened. The notion that, "If I knew why, then I would be okay," is the basis for the information-seeking behavior. The person's expectation is that information alone will reduce the uncertainty, and to a degree, it does so, but more information does not continue to reduce the uncertainty. As the person becomes aware of the consequences of the loss, uncertainty increases.

*Structuring for Certainty*

The bereaved person must now reduce the uncertainty engendered by the unknown future via processes described as "structuring for certainty." The purpose of this structuring is to create a new reality, since the person is now aware of the life transition. The certainty processes aid a person in identifying who she was at that pre-loss time, who he/she is at this time, and who she/he will be in the future. This sense of self, described as "identity constancy," is the stable condition of being oneself. Once a bereaved's reality has been disrupted, he/she becomes unsure and uncertain about identity. The formerly defined parameters are absent, modified, or changed in some manner. She must now reconstruct a new sense of self by the process of structuring for certainty. A process described as "regaining integrity," which is the awareness of physical durability, and ending the subjective experience of fragility, is a means of structuring for certainty. The feeling of being fragile blocks the awareness of the permanency of the loss, and hinders the transition. As one woman reported, "You can't be expected to do anything." Another woman reported that during the early period of separation from her husband, she needed to stay home a great deal, safely within the walls of her home, in order to feel less fragile. Trigger events will inform of the permanency of the loss, while simultaneously one is made aware of his/her fragility.

Fragility results from an injury/illness that makes a person uncertain about self and body, emotions, and even spirituality. The feeling of fragility may result from feeling physically, emotionally, spiritually or socially tenuous. The bereaved must develop to a sense of durability/intactness, which reduces uncertainty. The means of reducing or curtailing the fragility depends on the nature of the loss and the earlier sense of self.

A second process that structures for certainty is called, "cohort comparative testing." The value of support groups for patients in therapy is that these groups allow one to measure oneself against some identifiable model, and to note similarities and/or differences. The contrasts may be perceived in terms of such subjective experiences as fragility or missed options or reactivation. Women in a group, in therapy, or talking with a friend who has experienced a similar loss, will use such comparisons as a measure of their own progress. The only criterion for comparative testing is that the model one uses must have experienced the loss for a longer time that the individual responding to a loss. Eventually the person will even use herself as a model of comparison, observing, "In contrast to six months ago, I am now really.......!"

A third process that is important is "normalization," which involves engaging in behaviors that mirror the standard established by the core society. Returning to work is reported as being of significance in the recovery of a woman following the death of a spouse. The ability to respond positively to a friend who is the mother of a living child marks an important advance for a woman whose child has died. Wearing the same style of clothing that is popular with other teenagers is important to a spinal-cord injured teen. Eating out, entertaining, buying new clothes, going shopping, are part of normalizing one's life following a weight loss.

Another structuring process for certainty is "competency testing," determining the reestablishment of an attribute/skill previously claimed by the person prior to the disrupting event. Women who find that they retain certain skills, attractiveness, the ability to work and to comfort others, demonstrate the effectiveness of competency testing.

Activities in which an individual can no longer claim competency become missed options. A woman may utilize a number of strategies that lessen, substitute, delay, or redefine missed options. These strategies are described as "minimizing missed options." A woman who misses the sexual contacts provided by a no longer available lover/husband may supply the need for body contact/stimulation by using a substitute as such body massages. A woman whose education is disrupted by an illness may decide to delay that missed option. A woman who can no longer call her lover when she is out of town may decide to call her home answering service and leave a loving message to herself, and thus she redefines the missed option. Assisting women to minimize missed options in a myriad of ways is helpful. In fact, all the processes described as structuring for certainty may be used for intervention either with the woman herself or by persons who are interested in assisting the woman as she responds to a loss.

Finally, it is noted that patients may not acknowledge the disruptive event, and thus the subsequent restructuring of reality will not occur. It is further noted that they may not engage in processes to reduce the uncertainty following a loss. These are the people like women who wait for the husband to return even if he is remarried, or refuse to engage in rehabilitation therapy because -- as one client put it -- total body function would return despite her C5 fracture.

It is suggested that these patients are unable to realign their identity to congruence with the changes in their circumstances caused by the disrupting event, and consequently they remain in a reality that limits their engagement in living and in creating other possible realities. It may be that they are unable to find or create meaning in the event or are unable to neutralize the loss or to release the loss and its implication. This group has essentially taken time out from a shared reality with persons who recognize the changed circumstances.

The life transition theory is about people, who are responding to losses and engaging in the disruption that has occurred in order to create other possibilities for themselves outside the context of the loss. The closure of the life transition occurs when the person attends to aspects in her life that are not centered on the loss. The "loss" transition no longer takes priority over other possible transitions.

## Endnotes

1. The initiation of divorce proceedings or a commitment to lost weight are **determined decisions**. The death of one's child or the incurring of a spinal cord injury are examples of **a critical incident**.

2. No judgement is made whether this is desirable or undesirable.

3. For one woman, the determined decision to remove her wedding ring, long after divorce proceedings have been filed, initiates the life transition whereas another woman initiates the life transition when she first decides to divorce.

4. In any human context, there are multiple transitions. Discussions, unfortunately, are time and space bound within the confines of our language.

5. This is useless, because the pre-loss reality is not functional any more, and if she continues to engage in experiences as if the loss had not occurred, then she will not be engaging in active living.

# WOMAN, BODY IMAGE AND SELF-IMAGE
## Irene Seeland

In considering the impact of bodily damage to a woman, and to her own sense of self and her body image, we must define what we really mean by self-image and body image. What is a body image? It is a concept of our physical self. How do we achieve it? Babies don't have it, small children don't quite have it yet, but somewhere between late childhood and early adolescence, we become self aware. We look in the mirror and we see ourselves, and we compare ourselves with peers. We register feedback from others, and at some point, by the end of adolescence, we have formed a fairly specific image of our physical selves. We may be short and fat, or tall and strong, or thin and frail. We may be blond and beautiful, or pimply and straggly-haired; these points all comprise our image of our physical selves.

Obviously, our society assigns very specific values to body image, giving us specific clues as to what is acceptable and what is not. Most of us do not quite fulfill the ideal but we learn to live with the images that we encounter most of the time.

However it is not only what society presents as the ideal body image that determines our values. What we learn in interaction with others as we grow into adolescence, our first personal and intimate relationships, teach us a great deal about whether or not our physical being is acceptable or attractive. We learn to regard it as something that can either help or hinder us in our relationships with others.

We expect women to be, if not beautiful, at least attractive. We expect them to be soft-skinned and smooth, and well-built in a variety of ways. Women who cannot quite match those images begin to look elsewhere than their physical being for a sense of self and of identity. Such adjustment involves deficits as well as certain assets.

How does our body image feed into our self-image? How we see ourselves obviously involves more than merely physical perception. Are we nice people? Do we have a good character? What kind of temperament and intellectual capacities do we have? How successful are we in relating to people? All these factors contribute to our self-image.

If a large proportion of our self-image is dependent on our body image and it changes, our body image may exert a severe effect on our overall sense of self. When a child cuts his/her finger for the first time, a major shock is experienced, not simply from the pain, but from the fact that he or she can be physically traumatized, can bleed, is vulnerable. When most children, for the first time, experience a major shock; they are unable to leave the band-aid on. They must take it off and constantly examine the hurt area. It is as if they are saying "my God, this kind of thing can happen!" Thank goodness they learn that one heals, and the bruise disappears. The next time they know, by learning, that it is not so bad.

However the sense of our own mortality, vulnerability, and damaged integrity is transmitted by injury and trauma.

Clearly, in the whole field of cancer and cancer treatment, we deal with considerable trauma. At this point, the nature of our treatment is radical, meaning "tearing out at the roots," and that approach engenders a variety of implications. Here however, we will address specifically what women experience during the treatment of cancer, and only the cancer that is likely to be cured. Progressive and terminal illnesses bring many more factors into play, but these days, we can treat cancer so that a good number of women survive. Even though they earn normal long lives in terms of years, yet women can be devastated by the diagnosis of the cancer, and by the treatment that ensues.

Although similar effects are felt by men in comparable ways, we are here concerned with women and reactions specific for women because the injury, the trauma, is associated with body parts and body organs which carry special value for our gender. Damage to those organs exerts an impact, not only on body image, but very significantly on self-image, and on interrelationships with other people. Some of my observations are not new, but certain points should be underlined because they may help us to lead women to a better resolution. The process of grief and mourning necessarily follows an experience of trauma and injury.

One of the obvious and visible parts of a woman's body is her breasts. In our society, the breast is very much part of the sexual image; many teenagers worry about having breasts that are too small, too large, or not properly shaped. Some young women worry that their bodies cannot match social expectations. They respond to feedback from young men, from older men, from their own peers, as to whether or not they are living up to current expectations or standards.

What happens when a woman who is very actively involved in a normal life -- a marriage, or normal sexual relationship -- must undergo a mastectomy? The first time I learned about the nature of this loss was when I was doing a surgical rotation. A very attractive young black nurse, 30 years old, 3 years very happily married, with a very active social life, suddenly found a lump. She was smart enough to come to the hospital. At that point a radical mastectomy was the treatment of choice, and she knew that, and she consented to it. She was apparently quite prepared to deal with the situation. She experienced a totally uncomplicated surgery, she healed... according to the surgeons, "beautifully." Indeed, she had a "beautiful" scar, and we often talked about how "beautiful" her scar was. However, the part of me that is a woman, was very uncomfortable, because I realized that surgically I had made a beautiful scar, but it was only a scar, after all. If you have ever seen a female after a mastectomy, you know that the surgeon has removed most of the breast, the muscles, and the lymph nodes; what remains is basically a rib cage covered by skin. It is really horrendous to look at, even if it heals nicely.

We sent the patient home, terribly pleased with ourselves. She showed no positive lymph nodes; she had a very good prognosis for cure; and she seemed to be coping well. Six weeks later she arrived at the clinic for a follow-up and something was obviously very wrong. She had done her exercises, she had full mobility, she was obviously well healed and yet something was just very wrong. So I finally asked, What's happening in your life?" She burst into tears and started telling me how she had not been able to leave her house; how she had not dared to meet her friends who all know that she had a mastectomy; and how she felt extremely conspicuous. She thought everybody was going to stare at her, to try to see something. Her husband had not touched her, not just sexually, but hadn't touched her at all. She was taking showers in her slip. She just could not look at herself.

Clearly, this young woman, who had been physically extremely attractive, and whose body was a most important part of her self-image, had suffered an extreme trauma. The feedback from her husband delivered the message, "You are damaged goods, I won't have anything to do with you." She was quite frightened by the possibility of his leaving her for another woman. The problem was to find some way to reconstitute her life, to locate a way between the two of them to make this marriage work again.

We asked the husband to come in; we met with him individually, and we met with both of them. The psychiatrist worked with them for a period of several months, and began a process of resolution. I know the results of the long-term follow-up in this particular situation, but it struck home to me how devastating such an event may prove in the life of a young woman whose physical image was a highly significant part of her overall being. Other cases were somewhat different. Another patient had had radiation treatment and it developed into a chronic ulcerating scar. They finally found cancer tissue in the scar, so that she had to continue with more surgery. She developed a lymph swelling in the arm so large that she had to carry her arm in a sling, and the possibility arose that the doctors might amputate it because the patient was unable to function while carrying this tremendous burden.

Here was a woman who had been married for 30 years. The marriage was quite stable, and the couple had grown-up children. She was also well established in the community. Therefore, the impact of her condition on her relationship with her husband, and associates, although it was traumatic, obviously did not have the same effect as it did on the very young marriage described earlier. However, for her a major trauma was that she could no longer be and do what had given her a very strong sense of self. She was a fanatic gardener and was celebrated for the ST&T. She was also an active hostess. She invited many women to her home, talked with many people, and frequently volunteered in the community. Obviously, carrying this huge arm, she was unable to participate in such activities. The resulting frustration produced a tremendous amount of trauma, as well as rage; that not only had she endured a mastectomy, but she had to learn how to deal with these bizarre consequences as well. The side effects of this rage very nearly turned into a very ugly malpractice suit, not necessarily because there was malpractice, but because she had to somehow vent her rage somewhere.

Mastectomy is obviously a major trauma in a woman's life, more so, in our experience, with younger, sexually active women, women whose physical appearance is a major part of their self-image. One interesting phenomenon we found was that a woman 65 years old would care as much for her body image as a younger woman.

A lag time occurs between our real body and our self-image, as you must realize if you have looked in a shop window on the street and wondered, "Is that me? Is that chubby, middle-aged lady me? I'm charming and young and slim and I'm..." We have not quite integrated the fact of having moved on; we cannot yet deal with the reality of our ongoing life process. Even if a woman is not sexually active, sexual activity is meaningful to her and presents a confirmation of her womanhood, her femininity.

Another major area in which a woman clearly experiences major trauma is a hysterectomy, whether partial or total, the reaction understandable, since the surgery eliminates the ability to bear children; even if one is not planning to have children the potential is eliminated. In the past, society defined a woman's function as child-bearer to continue the human race; this attitude still must exist, because, otherwise, the race wouldn't persist. However, these days, women have found other avenues for self-esteem. Nevertheless something magical is attached to the capacity to have a child. The man contributes his equal share, but for nine months, the woman carries and nurtures the new life in a uniquely intimate relationship.

Consider our situation with a 13-year-old Chinese girl who came in with a rapidly growing ovarian tumor. Since it already involved the uterus, we performed a total hysterectomy. How do you explain the implications of such a procedure to a 13-year-old? She died so quickly that explanations never became an issue, but the situation created a trauma for everyone involved. We knew that, if she had lived, this young girl would never have had a normal female life. She would not menstruate, she could not conceive, she could not have children. Women who have borne children, healthy, alive and well, deal somewhat better with hysterectomy, and yet they report a deep sense of loss because even when you have all the children you want, you still want to retain your options.

Many women who experience menopause don't mind, in a certain way, losing their menses, yet they feel a loss of an essential part of themselves in losing the ability to bear children. Clearly, when the loss is precipitated by such a traumatic event as hysterectomy, the condition is much more difficult to cope with. A part of the woman's body that is meant to be creative is diseased, and many women have expressed particular distress that it is the creative part of the body that is cancerous.

In the light of the American Calvinist or Puritan backgrounds, some women speculate upon possible guilt: the cancer is regarded as punishment for something they have done. Such a reaction seems to span wide ethnic and social backgrounds, and it is very real for women who have felt guilty about something -- perhaps a past abortion or frequent sexual intercourse. It is important that they rid themselves of this guilt, and not interpret the illness and the surgery as punishment for their sins. You want to keep these issues in mind. Although they are not necessarily true for all women, they are something of which to be aware, and to try to address.

In cases of hysterectomy, an ensuing process of premature aging really can upset all these hormones if you have. We are presently working with a young woman of 36 who required a total hysterectomy, which involves removing the ovaries. That means this woman is entering menopause fifteen years before she should. Again, here is a very attractive woman, married to an older man to whom her beauty and her youth are very, very important. She knows about and fears the physical side-effects of her surgery, and even though her surgery is not for a life-threatening cancer. Her condition is severe endometriosis, and there seems to be no other course of treatment at this point. She is experiencing severe anxiety and depression, and it requires intensive mental health counselling to help her work through to some acceptance that she remains a person, despite the side effects of this operation.

Such cases emphasize the main consideration that emerged while I was working with these women. Those who have a focus or a purpose in their own lives that does not heavily depend on their body image have a better chance of recuperating and continuing their lives in a meaningful fashion. That doesn't mean that they do not experience trauma, that they don't mourn, or pass through all the stages that we know about, but they ultimately reconstitute their lives. On the other hand, women whose sexuality and child-bearing capacity have constituted a major, vital part of their existence, find difficulty in locating a new focus for self-expression and source of self-worth. It is essential that we try to understand what has been meaningful and important to these women throughout their lives, to help them find new purpose and meaning.

Let me conclude with a story that is not about a woman but about a young man, just to equalize our outlook somewhat. The issues remain the same: here was a 16-year-old adolescent, Puerto Rican boy, in his last year in high school, suffering from acute leukemia. After an illness of six months, he was now in the final stages of an extremely destructive disease. He had been a very handsome young man, involved in body-building, and being an adolescent, he was very proud of his strong, beautiful body. At this point, as a result of the steroids, the medication, the transfusions, the bleeding, the infections, the whole course of his disease, he had not only lost his hair, but his body had deteriorated markedly. He expressed anger and sadness, mourning, and the awareness that he was going to die. We talked about all these things, and then he performed for me a most meaningful action about a week before he died.

I would call every day or every other day for about a half an hour. We simply talked, and one day he started to talk about his life, going on for two hours, and I realized I could not leave. He had to finish talking. In those two hours, he spoke about all the things in his life that he felt good about, and some of them were very small things: how he was helpful to little old ladies; the night job he held as an elevator operator, and how he had been good at it. He had not "goofed off," and he had been kind to people -- he mentioned many such things, and at the end he said to me, "You know, I didn't have a lot of time, but I don't feel bad. I did the best I think I could," and I found myself hoping that I can say that when I go. He could say that at sixteen, and somehow his own sense of ego-integrity had superseded the physical deterioration, the illness, the impending death. Somehow he was able to find out who he was essentially, and discover that there had been meaning in his life, even if it only lasted for sixteen years, and was expressed to and "outsider."

This young man gave me a clue to how any of us who must encounter such trauma as the destruction of our body image, and alteration of our self-image, can ultimately survive by finding those aspects of ourselves which are eternal and essential, despite our limited, physical reality.

# LOVE SHOCK
# A STUDY OF THE PHENOMENA INVOLVED IN THE MANAGEMENT OF INDIVIDUALS FACING THE LOSS OF A LOVE RELATIONSHIP

### Stephen Viton Gullo
#### with the collaboration of Henry Berger

<u>Losing Someone You Love</u>

Working with bereaved people has taught me not only about the dynamics of loss and grief, but more important, about how men and women cope with the loss of love relationships. This paper shares some of the results derived from a study undertaken of anticipatory grief with colleagues such as Dr. Henry Berger of the New York Hospital-Cornell Medical Center. We achieved insight into a universal and especially human aspect of bereavement -- the loss of a loved person, not by death, but by separation and divorce.

Studies of the grief experience, pioneered by Doctors Lindeman, Weissman, Parkes, and others, have probed deeply into the results of losing a loved person through death. Our investigation focused on another phenomenon, the experience of losing a person who still lives. What is the cost of this experience? How do people cope with it? How can you help them to facilitate and overcome the resulting pain of this experience, and even to grow through it.

How does losing someone through the termination of a relationship, a divorce or a separation differ from loss by death? A critical difference is that although we may lose a person, he or she continues to exist in reality; we are continually forced to confront this person's existence.

The second significant element is that of personal rejection: whether you are the person who is rejected or the individual who decides to terminate a relationship, you must live with feelings, not only of loss but often of a sense of failure, or rejection, and guilt. The situation is complicated by the fact that much of the reaction to this loss may be colored by the actions of the other person. If an ex-partner is luxuriating in a Sutton Place apartment, or vacationing on the Cote D'Azur with a new mate, this fact will dramatically affect your response to the personal loss.

The work of Dr. Michael Liebowitz and Dr. Donaldo Klein at Columbia also suggests that a specific chemical in the brain may be associated with being "in love," possibly phenylethlamine (a compound related to amphetamines). Such studies suggest that when we are in the state of "love" or of "falling in love," the production of these neuro-chemicals appears to increase dramatically and when we are withdrawing from a love relationship, we not only must deal with a psychological component, but probably also with a physiological component that contributes to feelings of distress. High levels of these neurochemicals appear to be correlated with feelings of well-being, elation, or what some would call the "love high." When the chemicals dramatically decrease, feelings of emotional pain and depression are intensified.

## The "Love Shock" Experience

As I studied women who had lost a husband, I heard again and again such statements as, "I knew he was dying. I knew the end was near, but when it happened, I was in shock. I couldn't believe it. Never again to hear his voice, to see his face, or to touch him. The finality was difficult to comprehend." Working with people who had come through a divorce, and with lovers who had decided to separate, I again heard the same expressions of shock and numbness, and observed a sense of "loss and wondering" when a significant relationship finally came to an end.

Studying these phenomena of shock and disorientation that characterize these losses parallel the reactions of combat soldiers who have experienced shell shock. Here, too is the sense of emotional disorientation, withdrawal, hesitancy to come close to others for fear of losing them, sleep and eating disorders, grief, and most of all, a feeling of "emotional numbness" and shock over what has happened: the near loss of life itself. From these similar responses to lost love and to shell shock, emerges the concept of "love shock." A technical definition of the term would be the state of psychological disorientation and numbness, characterized by feelings of profound loss, emptiness and yearning, precipitated by the termination of a significant relationship.

My colleague, Dr. Berger, stresses that the person who initiates the break-up of a love relationship may suffer as much "love shock" as the person who is rejected, if not more. As we studied love relationships, we frequently found that the person who ended the relationship often did so in anticipation of the other partner acting first, or because the profound dissatisfaction with or pain of the relationship could no longer be tolerated.

## The Stages of Love Shock

The experience of love shock appears to follow a definite course. Certain stages of the loss experience may be shock, grief, blame, magnification, resignation, renewal, and "goodbye."

The first stage is characterized by a sense of numbness, of wondering, of a void, of having lost a part of oneself. One of our patients was at home when she received a phone call from her husband saying that he had been re-evaluating their relationship in light of some of the talks they had had about separating. He had decided that it was right for them to divorce and he was leaving tomorrow. At that moment, this woman described feeling a sense of "numbness ... a feeling of time stopped," and the only vivid picture she has in her mind to this day, five years later, was of the open window, and wanting to jump. This was the only man with whom she had been intimate in her life, and for thirty years, this man had been the basis of her whole existence. At the moment he stated, "It's over," she felt as if part of her own body had been "ripped away." At the moment when she was confronted with that decision, she experienced a sense of shock and numbness, as well as a fear of the unknown.

The second stage is the grief stage, occurring with the loss of someone you love, whether through death, divorce, or separation. If this person is significant to your internal stability, it is normal to expect a period of mourning. It is normal to desire, in some way, to be reunited with this person. In cases where the relationship was dissatisfying, mourning may take a more intricate course. One may mourn for all the time and psychic energy that was invested fruitlessly, or for the promise of what could have been. Or one may mourn for the "role loss" rather than for the lost person, e.g., no longer being a wife, but a single person alone in the world again.

Indeed, some of the most "grief stricken" individuals I've worked with had emerged from very unsatisfactory relationships. A widow's hysteria may be related more to feelings of material loss and insecurity than to the passions of lost love. Other significant symptoms characterize this second stage. Love shock victims often experience obsessional thinking about their former lover, constantly wondering what they are doing, constantly longing in someway to restore the relationship.

The next stage can be identified as magnification. When a love relationship has been dissolved, one person frequently magnifies, beyond the boundaries of reality, the positive aspects of the lost partner's new situation. "He must be having such a great time. He must be with a new partner who is so beautiful, so rewarding to be with, whereas I am suffering pain and rejection." This magnification functions also in the tendency to idealize how smoothly the life of the lost person is now proceeding while one's own life is shattered. Another form of magnification concerns the former partner's personality: the grieving individual may block out all negative memories, or may block out any positive aspects of the lost partner.

The third condition is the blame stage. Most frequently, people blame the loss of a love relationship on one of three factors: the other person, circumstances (including another involvement), or on a career, with or without the demands of traveling.

It is frequently amazing how little anger some people feel. In spite of inflicted hurt, in spite of the sense of failure, a deep caring for the other person often continues. I recently had the opportunity to work with the wife of one of America's leading personalities who was going through a divorce. She might have said much that would have destroyed his career, or used this information as a bargaining chip in terms of the financial settlement. Her own conscience would not permit such behavior, despite evidence of his frequent infidelities.

The next stage of the love shock phenomenon is resignation. When people have made a deep commitment and they have worked at it, they cannot part with it easily. They resign themselves to the failure rather than accept it. But the resignation is enormously important to admitting reality. After shock, mourning, and magnification, finally reality asserts itself as one accepts the fact that the relationship is over, and it cannot exist again.

The final two stages can be identified as renewal and the "goodbye" stage. In the stage of renewal, the person begins to pull together the shattered pieces of his or her life and ego. He or she begins once again to be interested in dating. I call the initial phase of dating, "comparison dating." Anyone who has experienced the break-up of a love relationship that mattered deeply finds himself or herself initially comparing the person being dated to the former partner. This may not be entirely true to the "data," but it is an entirely normal part of the process of love shock. The renewal stage is marked by the reemergence of risk-taking behavior; "to love takes courage." After being hurt or scarred, after living with a sense of failure, to once again become this vulnerable does take bravery.

The final stage is the "goodbye" stage. Resignation is the stage where the person intellectually recognizes that the love relationship has come to an end. In the "good bye" stage, the person has resumed a normal social life and can finally let go, both psychologically and emotionally, without severe pain. It is not only an intellectual experience, but a psychic, emotional experience as well. It is a "closing of the door" on all that has been.

The person loses intense interest in what the lost partner is doing, nor desires to see that person. In the words of Freud, he or she has become "emotionally detached." By emotional decathexis, Freud meant the withdrawal of psychic energy and bond from one person or valued object, so that one would again be free to invest it in another. Perhaps the Jewish concept of the "Kaddish," the prayers said for a deceased loved one, is appropriate here. In the "good bye" stage, the person is finally able to say Kaddish for the relationship and forget what has been most significant. He or she can now go forward without impairment.

One issue in dealing with the love shock experience is whether it is possible to anesthetize a human being against some of the psychic pain of loss. I believe strongly that tragedy exists in human life and that neither extensive therapy nor drugs can remove the pain inherent in living.

However, I certainly do believe that through love shock therapy, we can help. We have particularly addressed these issues since we are dealing with critical therapeutic questions in two dimensions: a) can we reduce the intensity of this pain, and, b) can we accelerate the painful process of withdrawal from a love relationship? The answer to both of these questions, in most cases, is "yes". We have developed some techniques to take people through this crisis period in life.

Cassette Therapy

A key element is the use of cassettes, specifically to gradually bring the love shock victim to a confrontation with his or her painful memories of the lost love relationship, to facilitate the grief work, and to minimize the pain endured. In this way a sense of self can be rebuilt and the process of withdrawing may be enabled without accompanying pathological symptoms and without inhibiting the normal process.

The use of cassettes is particularly helpful in four ways: first, it enables us to intensify the therapy, since the person can listen to the therapeutic message again and again, facilitating insight and healing. Second, it enables the patient to activate therapy concurrent with times of greatest pain and stress, for example, at night and weekends, when the patient may feel most lonely. Third, it increases the time efficiency of therapy. The ability of patients to "bring home" and review therapeutic insights minimizes the "forgetting" of painful material and maximizes corrective suggestions. It also serves as a motivation and a reminder that the pain will pass.

Students of history know that the Victorian period was an age of unresolved mourning dominated by a grieving Queen who disappeared from public view for more than two decades. It was only on the jubilee of her coronation, that the "Widow of Windsor" reluctantly agreed to reappear. We do not wish our patients to become Queen Victorias, carrying with them emotional scars that may create a phobic fear of loving. One of the principal characteristics of schizoid or schizophrenic behavior is the fear of intimacy. So often, when a person has been hurt in a love relationship, he or she experiences such a period and it is most critical to overcome this fear; to "immunize" the patient against the love phobia which could easily develop.

Through the use of audio cassettes, one additional goal is facilitated: education. Our work is truly a teaching therapy, not psychotherapy for psychopathology. The experience of "love shock" is a normal and almost universal one. We are dealing with a normal process; trying to mitigate its pain and facilitate its course. Love shock is not a pathological state. Indeed, it is not the shock and grief of such reaction that bodes ill for patients' mental and physical welfare. The cassette serves as a continuing teacher, encouraging the person to talk of the lost love, as well as taking away a positive learning experience, not just a negative and painful one.

## The Process of Love Shock Therapy

We do not insist that the patient throw out the pictures, the love notes, and the gifts. These objects are truly what Volkan has called "linking objects." In the patients that we have studied, these objects create a link between themselves and their lost persons, and we do not want them to discard this link until they have dealt cognitively and effectively with the fact that the relationship has ended, why it has ended, and how to complete the unfinished business of loving. Frequently when a love relationship ends, ego, pride, hurt, and anger block expression. We insist that the patients complete the unfinished business of loving, however painful it may be.

They begin by saying to us what they would have said to the lost partner. This function is not an end in itself, but supplies a bridge which hopefully will enable them to speak more freely to the person they have lost as well as to the next person with whom they may share an intimate relationship. We insist that they bring with them a personal statement about why they loved this person and why the love relationship came to an end. We insist that they also include any pictures or special moments of the relationship.

As the therapy progresses, the tapes are changed to relate to the different stages through which the person is passing. One of the phenomena we emphasize is the role of "magnification." I am constantly amazed at the capacity for self-delusion in love relationships that are ongoing, as well as those ending. So often women speak of their husbands as very caring or loving. Often they assume blame for a break-up themselves, when the truth was the opposite. The human mind blocks out pain and retains that which is positive. Problems arise when this quality interferes with our functioning. I have no particular fondness for reality. (I often tell my patients that it matters less to be "normal" then to be happy!)

In the break-up of love relationships, often a peculiar form of amnesia blocks out the negative to suppress pain. But pain is also a teacher. We should not block it out before we have learned from it. Because the tapes both support the patient's ego, and force him or her to confront certain issues at the appropriate time, they help with the process of withdrawing from the love relationship.

As the process continues, we enter a period of rebuilding. It is one thing to suffer a loss and to cope with it; it is another matter to resume living and loving. We focus on building new social relationships and developing a sense of confidence and renewal. I can postulate from my work with bereaved people that there is a time to heal, to live again. We encourage this natural drive in the patient, and, where anger is appropriate, to help him or her separate from the lost person, we also use and encourage this emotion.

In the final phase of our work, we ask the patient to draw up a balance sheet of what he or she took from the relationship that was positive, and what it cost him or her emotionally. We insist on this balance sheet as a final reckoning of what the relationship both gave and took from the patient's life.

Final sessions are devoted to the phenomenon we call "good-bye." We know from thanatology research how critical it is for the dying patient and loved ones to complete the business of living and say "good-bye." And so it is in our love relationships. We must be able to acknowledge both the negative and the positive elements that existed and to recognize that this is a situation from which we must separate.

In the final statement on the balance sheet, one of my patients wrote, "I have not failed you, and you have not failed me. We are children of two different worlds and we must find in those worlds, the love, the support, the companionship that we could never give to one another." More than anything else that I can say, these lines summarize the psychological process of letting go -- to view the person that you loved not just with anger or with hatred (if that is appropriate), but also (if it is appropriate) with caring and positive feelings.

Our strategy derives from Freud's theory of object decathexis. He maintained that psychic energy is limited, rather than infinite. To be able to proceed to the next love relationship, we must be able to withdraw our commitment (decathex) from the original one.

A Final Perspective

In Kubler-Ross's book, "Death the Final Stage of Growth," Beatrice Meize wrote of the death of her son, that she was filled with "numbness," with pain, and sense of wandering. I can tell you from a decade of research in clinical work with the victims of love loss, that when a love relationship comes to an end, we see the same phenomena, which we have termed "love shock."

No experience in human life is more central and universal than loss. It begins with the loss of our pets, of our grandparents, of our youth, and as we get older, our loved ones, our health, and ultimately, our own lives. In fact, the only certainty in life is loss. Coping with it is critical not only for our patients, but for our own growth.

**REFERENCES**

Gullo, Stephen. "Games Children Play in Coping and Facing Death," Keynote address, Symposium on "The Child and Death", sponsored by Foundation of Thanatology, Columbia-Presbyterian Medical Center, January 1979.

Blackwell, Robert, Pub. The Fighter's Guide to Divorce, Chicago, Regnery, 1977.

Bohannon, Paul, ed. Divorce and After: An Analysis of the Emotional and Social Problems of Divorce, Garden City: Doubleday, 1971.

Bowlby, John, Attachment and Loss, Vol. 1, Attachment. New York: Basic Books, 1969.

Jones, Eve, Raising Your Child In A Fatherless Home. London: Collier-Macmillan, 1963.

Kübler-Ross, Elizabeth, Death: The Final Stage of Growth. New Jersey: Prentice-Hall, 1974.

Lindemann, Erich, Symptomology and Management of Acute Grief. In Parad, H.H., ed. Crisis Intervention. Selected Readings, New York: Family Service Association of America, 1965.

Marris, Peter. Loss and Change. New York; Pantheon, 1974.

Martin, John R. Divorce and Remarriage: A Perspective of Counseling. Scottsdale:Herald Press, 1974.

Parkes, Colin Murray. Bereavement: Studies of Grief in Adult Life. New York: International Universities Press, 1972.

Weisman, Avery. On Dying and Denying, New York: Behavioral Publications, 1972.

## SOCIAL ASPECTS OF SEXUAL LOSS: A RADICAL ESSAY
### David Wendell Moeller, Ph.D.

> ...lust assumes power not only over the whole body, and not only from the outside, but also internally; it disturbs the whole man, when the mental emotion combines and mingles with the physical craving resulting in a pleasure surpassing all physical delights. So intense is the pleasure that when it reaches its climax, there is an almost total extinction of mental alertness; the intellectual sentries, as it were are overwhelmed.
>
> *St. Augustine*

A 48-year-old woman sat in her hospital bed in her private room, tears swelling in her eyes and terror in her face. She had recently returned from surgery, where a radical mastectomy had been performed. The pain of loss, the indescribable hurt of seeing one side of her chest flat and scarred in a society where breasts are important to the definition of a woman's sexuality and hence to her personhood -- this pain was pulsating through her body and her mind.

The depth of this woman's suffering is far beyond my ability to articulate. Her sense of despair was overwhelming. The life she had known for 48 years had been decimated in a few short hours by her surgeon's scalpel. The remote awareness of "Yes, I know that someday I will die" had been transformed by her cancer into keen and pressing anticipatory fear: "I may die very soon. Oh my God, is it really possible that this is death?"

In a very real way this woman had developed an acute plethora of needs for support, fellowship, solace and comfort. These needs, however, remained largely unfulfilled throughout the her hospitalization. Her physicians, in the name of technique, objectivity, scientific method or whatever the prevailing excuse is for not caring today, depersonalized their "management" of this patient to the extent that the essential qualities and needs of her humanity were ignored and overlooked.

The frustration and anger brewing within this patient found expression in the seemingly interminable questions she asked her physicians. She relentlessly pursued this strategy of reliving or at least expressing her fears and anxieties and was promptly labeled as uncooperative, demanding, and overemotional. Indeed, her surgeon returned from her bedside and a postoperative examination and exclaimed to all present in the doctor's lounge: "I really don't see what she's angry about. She has a perfectly healed wound."

The foregoing description is not a metaphorical statement, but rather a summary of the realities of the medical neglect of the personal and social needs of seriously ill patients. In this vein, this paper will address the underlying societal factors that give rise to neglectful treatment of women patients suffering from sexual loss. The discussion will be limited specifically to women suffering from cancer who in addition to their sexual loss, are confronting the prospect of dying.

In 1932, Huxley unveiled his vision of a future utopia; a *Brave New World* where human inclinations and concerns are mastered through the "Holy Spirit" of technology. In his grand society, suffering was expunged from human experience by medical triumphs, behavioral conditioning, and the widespread dissemination of the all-important Soma. Soma, more effective than valium, bourbon, or heroin without the harmful effects of these drugs, offered the citizens of Brave New World a vacation from reality upon demand. In short, soma offered each citizen protection from any semblance of suffering.

Freud would be interested to know that in Huxley's fantasy utopia, sex was unrestricted except for the single stipulation that it not involve intimacy, loving, or concern for one's partner. Wide-spread and permissive sexual activity was encouraged as a sanctuary; pleasure a substitute for human warmth and fellowship. An endless stream of impersonal orgasms did not interfere with a person's commitment to the principals of efficiency, progress, and production which highlighted the technological foundation of the new world. A loving and caring ethos would have been expensive in terms of its absorption of time and energy depletion. It would have lessened citizens' commitment to the technological fabric of Huxley's society. Hence, to protect the sanctity of the technological impulse, affectivity and human interconnection had to be nullified. Love was produced out of existence; technology reigned over human life.

Huxley also saw the realities of human dying as potentially disastrous to the societal texture of his standardized, harmonious utopia. The suffering associated with dying, whether it occurs in anticipation of one's own death or through witnessing the death of another, can be awesome enough to reduce the behavior of the sanest men and women to that of savages. It is not surprising then that in *Brave New World*, death conditioning was a salient tool of everyday socialization. In order for life to be made free of suffering, emotionally neutral, and in order for technology to reign over everyday life, the experience of dying had to be removed from the realm of the terrible. Each child, therefore, was successfully desensitized to human dying with the single purpose of obliterating the subjective human dimension of suffering from life. In the final analysis, dying became and remained an issue of technical management, to be left to the technicians of the Hospital for Dying. Thus, death was transmuted into an emotionally neutral event, never sufficiently poignant to interrupt the next orgy, meal, or Soma holiday.

In short, the technostructure of *Brave New World*, successfully monopolized the very experience of being human. The subjective human qualities of joy and suffering were cast aside in favor of the standardization of life. The need and drive to feel was quelled by "the feelies," movie-like happenings that fabricated and replicated every dimension of life. Henceforth, individuals would not need to experience passion, fear, love, anger, or anxiety because these factors could be "had" at any time at the "feelies." Indeed, Huxley's *Brave New World* accomplished unequaled transcendence over the human condition through technological progress. (Unfortunately, however, the woman whose case summary began this essay had not been able to limit the requirements of her humanity to the strictures of the technological ethos.)

Huxley's fictitious society has special significance in relation to current American realities and to the issue of women and loss. Perhaps the most penetrating discussion of the American version of his world can be found in Ellul's (1964) monograph, *The Technological Society*, in which he discusses the role of technique in modern civilization. As Ellul defines it, technique is a societal orientation towards the value of efficiency and reason. It is the "totality of methods or ways of acting, rationally arrived at and having absolute efficiency in every area of human activity." The point Ellul drives home is that virtually no aspect of human life, in a modern society can escape technique. From the organization of the state and economy, to the manipulation of human beings through advertising, education, and medical procedures, technique is the value underlying and unifying all activity. To touch the plane of human reality for a moment, it is not difficult to see how sexual activity, making and saving money, meeting people, having fun, losing weight, running for political office, and killing others in warfare are coordinated by the calculus of efficiency and rationality. It is within this technical framework that we need to understand the surgeon's losing sight of the importance of the subjective needs of his mastectomy patient.

Another prominent societal factor that affects the issue of women and loss is the cultural foundation of hedonism, which serves to create societal images of beauty and to cast sexuality into the mold of a "consumable commodity." To illustrate the connection between American civilization and the tragedy of physical disfigurement and death, the role of sexual pleasure in everyday life must be noted. The point I advance is that sexual hedonism is so central to American living that any sustained interference with the pursuit of this pleasure becomes intolerable to the modern American mentality.

The emphasis on sexuality can be found in virtually every corner of our culture. The focus on fashions and cosmetics, the pursuit of beauty and perfection of sexual techniques testify to importance of a sexual self-image in the American character. It should be immediately recognized that sex is not just a compartmentalized component of life here, but rather has penetrated deeply into the corpuscles of the American bloodstream. Our humor, art, films, novels and commercials are all deeply touched by sexual stimuli. It is precisely this realization, that sex and artifacts of sex dominate modern consciousness, which pinpoints the fact that important portions of our individual identity and personhood are shaped and defined by sexual dimensions.

Physical beauty is inherent in the successful pursuit of the hedonistic ethic. However, a primary obstacle to becoming beautiful and enticing and to finding an equally beautiful, enticing partner is that these qualities are rare in American culture. Ideal images of the sexual being (and hence, the adequate personal and social being) have been formulated and continually presented to the American public by the mass media. The images that have been created are so tantalizing, mysterious, and sensual that they are, in reality, unattainable by ordinary folk. These images represent the ultimate ideal of what our hedonistic civilization can achieve. In short, in our society, sexual satisfaction has become a precious and rare commodity because ordinary people find it essentially impossible to approximate the images that emanate from "the cult of the beautiful."

Because sexuality is a scarce commodity, as it should ideally be in a hedonistic society, its value increases. The more scarce a thing is, the more its value increases and the harder people strive for it. The pursuit of sexiness and beauty is therefore a basic motivational force in American culture. As a result of the intensity of the struggle to become beautiful and sexually alluring, the character of our culture revolves around the pursuit and attainment of these qualities. This is especially true for women. In American society, the female search for identity often originates and terminates in sexual factors. To the degree that a woman identifies her personhood with her sexuality, she reduces herself to a commodity to be evaluated and rated in a market place. Despite the supposed emancipation of these times, sex remains a central variable that defines, to a great extent the social identity of American women.

The loss of physical normalcy radically interrupts the pursuit of the underlying socio-sexual ideals of America, and becomes a social enemy. A woman who has channeled her self development through sexual variables will naturally feel blemished and inadequate when physical loss and dying scar her self image. It is in this vein that I argue that loss becomes so disruptive and frightening that it assumes the status of a social evil for American women.

Dying in an ugly, deteriorative way blemishes scientific technical omnipotence and threatens the hedonistic base of American culture. Whereas death is a central experience upon which traditional cultures and religious ways of life are based, dying and death are warts on the ideal of scientific and sexual perfection. A woman who is dying and who has become ugly in the process, becomes an inadequate human being. She has failed the gods of technique and narcissism. Although she is not responsible for her dying, her predicament violates sacred, societal values.

Social evil is culturally relevant in time and place, and will be defined here as violation of social ideals. Evil is not inherent in acts themselves, but rather is defined by the social response to specific qualities or behaviors. What then is the difference between social deviance and social evil? The important difference is one of qualitative degree. The qualities of dying are certainly more repulsive to the American way of life than addiction. Death carries connotations of wrongness, badness, and undesirability. Social evil elicits awe and fear in those it touches. It is strongly threatening to the prevailing sensibilities of a culture. Perhaps women who undergo physical deterioration in the process of dying experience the quintessential American encounter with human suffering.

A parody on the words of St. Augustine may be especially illuminating. His description of the evil of lust which began this presentation, provides an accurate base for describing the turmoil of physical decimation and the prospect of dying from cancer. Notice that only five of the original words need to be changed:

> This cancer assumes power over the whole body, and not only from the outside, but also internally; it disturbs the whole person, when emotion combines and mingles with the physical disturbance, it results in a pain surpassing all physical suffering. So intense is the pain that when it reaches its climax there is an almost total extinction of mental alertness; the intellectual sentries, as it were, are overwhelmed.

Encounters with women suffering from loss and impending death the social evil that women are enduring, at this very moment, in medical centers throughout the country, consider, for example, a twenty-two year old woman who had a four-year history of lymphoma. Her disease had spread until she had lumps on her vagina, under her arms, and on her head, some of them the size of golf balls. She commented on how these and other physical changes, loss of hair and weight, had affected her perceptions of herself. The scene she described took place nine months before her death:

> I became very self conscious. In fact a girl friend talked me into going out to a bar one night. I really didn't want to go. I was actually scared of going. When we were there and standing at the bar, a guy touched my hair and said, "Oh, is that a wig?" And I said, 'yes,' and jokingly he said, "What are you, bald?" Well, I just came home and I bawled my eyes out. That just killed me. It all just makes me feel so unfeminine, not me.

Another woman, 64 years old commented,

> I used to have such nice skin. Now look at me (she pointed to hair growth from chemotherapy on her face). My physician knew that this was going to happen to me and he went ahead and did it anyway. This is one thing you should tell all of your students: tell them medicine just doesn't care about what happens to us. Tell them, that they can't be trusted...
>
> Continuing she said, simply, "It just kills me for my husband to see me this way."

A 33 year-old woman shared her terrifying experience of having a breast removed. She died five months after this conversation took place.

> The missing breast is always on my mind. Even when I'm making love to my husband, I can't help but think that this just isn't me. It gives me such a headache that I always feel terrible afterwards.

This same patient went on to describe feeling inadequate because she couldn't wear the same kind of clothes she used to when she was normal and healthy. "I'm just not myself anymore, sexywise or bodywise. I'm just not who I used to be."

Another woman in her forties said:

> The sexual problems are immense. I feel totally helpless, blemished. I don't blame my husband. He feels guilty and unfulfilled. We really can't talk about it honestly. The emptiness looms. I just wish something could be done.

The relevant factor in this discussion is that there is little purpose or meaning in all of this suffering. The dying woman, burdened with physical deterioration, finds herself a prisoner of a societal values complex that is failing her in her time of human need. This is precisely the point that needs to be emphasized: the extremities of suffering experienced by women in the face of loss and dying are a social issue spawned by the society in which the women live.

As Huxley's *Brave New World* transmuted the human problems of living and dying into problems of technical management, so too does the American version of a technological society. The subjective fears and pains of women suffering through loss and dying cannot engage the energies of the technical society and its technocrats. Thus, the entire spectrum of socio-human needs of dying women becomes compressed into a regimen of patient management that is narrowly focused on the objective treatment of physical disease or symptoms. The callous neglect of physicians and the medical care system for the human vulnerabilities and needs of women facing loss and dying is an understandable by-product of technological values. Physicians, it must be remembered, are agents of this society; their task is to carry forth the technological imperatives, not to create their own version of caring for patients. Thus, physicians who live according to their role definition, and training, "should be" neglectful of the human suffering of these women.

In addition, the consequences of the neglect of the emotional needs of women patients is exacerbated by the fact that these women have become the pariahs of modern society. They are not only insisting on dying, but have become contaminated commodities in the hedonistic marketplace of sexual perfection. Hence, lack of support for their needs becomes even more vital in the face of their loss of identity. The degradation women do indeed suffer in the face of the social evil of loss and dying represents a devaluation of human life by society.

The task before Americans and the medical profession is to establish a new balance between the technical and the human spheres of knowledge. A balance must be established between humanity's capacity for love and fellowship and its capacity for neglect, greed, and self-involvement. The scales must be tipped in favor of love, community, and being human. To force in society is to continue to stet the degradation of women in the shadow of loss and dying and to heighten their suffering.

Perhaps, when all is said and done, it is the simple utopian solutions that are most workable and desirable. In "The Dreams of a Ridiculous Man," Dostoyevsky (1961) shows us really how simple the solution is:

> The key phrase is "Love others as you love yourself." And that's all there is to it. Nothing else is required. That would settle everything. Yes, of course it's nothing but an old truth that has been repeated and re-read a million times -- and still hasn't taken root.

But, if everyone wanted it, everything could be arranged immediately. Women facing loss and death need and deserve nothing less.

## References

Dostoyevsky, F. 1961. The Dream of a Ridiculous Man. New York: Signet.

Ellul, J. 1964. The Technological Society. New York: Vintage Books.

From, M.E. 1971. To Have or to Be. New York: Bantam Books.

Lasch, C. 1978. The Culture of Narcissism. New York: W.W. Norton and Co.

Roszak, T. 1969. The Making of a Counter Culture. New York: Doubleday and Co.

St. Augustine, 1972. Concerning The City of God: Against the Pagans. (H. Betterson- Trans). D. Knowles, ed. Harmondsworth: Penguin.

Huxley, A. L. 1932. Brave New World. New York: Harper and Row.

# THE CHANGING STATUS OF WOMEN IN THE PROFESSIONS
Meta Goswami

Examination of literature reveals that the participation of women in the labor force has increased over the years. The proportion of females who are in the labor force has increased from 28% to 36%. With the exception of the World War II period, the increase in female participation has been linear. Recent figures show an increase to 37.9% in 1974, 50.1% in 1978 and 51.6% in 1980.

Various social and political factors have contributed to this rise in the labor force with a correlative increasing status of women all over the world. Because of lowered infant mortality, women do not have to produce as many children as they did in the past. Increasing life expectancy makes more years available for productive living and contributions to society. Escalating costs and a higher standard of living make it necessary for women to contribute to the family's financial resources. A crucial variable is the rise of the democratic egalitarian ideology in modern as well as traditional societies. Increased educational attainment and employment opportunities have been particularly important in explaining the increase of women in the labor force.

Although the participation of women in the labor force has increased, their distribution in the professions remains low in comparison with the men. In 1900, women earned 6% of all Ph.D. degrees. By 1920, this proportion had reached 15% (U.S. Dept. of Labor, 1969). In 1978, 13% of the life scientists represented in the national sample (U.S. Bureau of the Census), were women. Among the physical scientists, 8% were women. In 1980, the proportion of all Ph.D.'s among women was 30% (National Academy of Sciences, 1972-1981). Women earned 22.6% of science and engineering doctorates in 1980 and may be expected to earn 35% to 40% by 1989 (National Center for Educational Statistics, 1980).

Sex-typing of occupations was described by Robert Merton. Occupations can be described as sex-typed when a very large majority of those in them are of one gender and when there is an associate normative expectation that this is as it should be.

Sex-typing occurs in all cultures. There is evidence of inter-occupational as well as intra-occupational sextypification. Medicine, dentistry, and engineering are male occupations, whereas social work, nursing, and teaching in grade school are female occupations. U.S. Census figures show that the dominant occupation groups for women were clerical or service work. The employment growth in these two areas has been primarily in traditionally female occupations (e.g. secretarial, typing, and health service work). In 1978, women comprised 81.3% of the workers in all health services occupations but only 11.3% were physicians (Bureau of Labor Statistics, 1979). The figure for women remained unchanged in 1980.

Sex-typing of work is even observed within professions, as in the case of medicine where women physicians tend to go into such specialties as pediatrics, psychiatry, and public health (Kosa and Coker, 1965). In 1977, specialties most commonly chosen by women were pediatrics (14.2%), internal medicine (12.6%), psychiatry (8.4%), general practice (8.1%), 5.3% of women were in obstetrics/gynecology and 9% in urology. In 1980, the order was internal medicine (16.5%), pediatrics (15.3%), psychiatry (9.7%), and obstetric/gynecology (6.0%) (A.M.A., 1979, 1981).

The three specialties most commonly chosen by men have been surgery, general (family) practice and internal medicine (Kehrer, 1974). In 1980, the ratio has changed to rank internal medicine first, then surgery, and general practice (A.M.A., 1981).

Various personal, social, economic, and political factors operate to contribute to the predominance of one sex in a particular occupation, with an associated societal expectation that this is how it should be. Early role learning in the socialization process plays an important part in womens' lack of interest in exploring opportunities as well as their lack of initiative (Dahlstrom, 1971). Sex-typing of occupations or the lower status of women within occupations could be a realistic adjustment for women who believe that extra-professional roles may impinge on professional role performance if they commit themselves to a demanding profession, or to a higher position with greater responsibility (Kosa and Coker, 1965).

Sex-typing may also be a consequence of a shared belief that certain traits which are feminine such as selflessness, compliance, tolerance, patience, and empathy, are more suitable for certain jobs like nursing, teaching, and social work and so women are counselled to take up these traditional supportive roles such as school teacher, clerk or hygienist by family, career counselors, and teachers. Men, on the other hand, are expected to be aggressive, competitive, independent and analytical, and are perceived to be better suited to those occupations that require detachment, analytical objectivity, and object orientation such as science and law. This mode of thinking however, does not take into consideration the fact that there could be as much variation within the sexes as between them (Hennig and Jardin, 1974; Bernard, 1971; Maccoby, 1963; Rossi, 1967). Interestingly, some authors have suggested that with rapid social change and sharing of roles, sex typification in tasks may greatly be reduced (Booth, 1972; Bernard, 1971).

Consequences of Sex-Typing

Sex-typing of occupations may have diverse consequences both at the individual level and the global level. Individuals of the "wrong gender" in a sex-typed occupation may have problems interacting with fellow students, colleagues, and consumers of services, as a result of perceived incongruent status. At the societal level, sex-typing gets in the way of finding the most qualified individual for the job, leading to under-utilization of talent and is therefore not in the best interest of society.

There is also a correlation between sex-typing and the prestige of a profession. All available evidence suggests that women are disproportionately concentrated in the marginal professions rather than the prestigious professions, and tend to settle down in the lower echelons, not only in the United States but in other countries as well.

Despite legislative and radical social change in countries such as Sweden and Russia, women still tend to settle in the lower spectrum of the occupational hierarchy and are disproportionately represented in the lower paying, lower prestige jobs (Galenson, 1973). Within occupations, positions that require more responsibility and decision-making and have a high financial remuneration are male dominated (Navarro, 19773). These positions are also more prestigious. Our observation that primary school teachers are mostly women whereas school principals are generally men, that women are disproportionately represented in the field of social work but the higher level administrative positions in this area are generally occupied by men is corroborated by findings from other studies (Grimm and Stern, 1974; Stamm, 1969). In America even though women dominate in the occupational groups of sewers and stitchers, tasks designated as "female" such as cooking and sewing, are still assigned to men in prestigious hotels and in the field of fashion designing.

In the field of medicine, surgery, which enjoys high prestige and is also highly remunerative, has proportionately more men than women whereas psychiatry, pediatrics, and public health which enjoy less prestige and less financial rewards, attract relatively more women. According to the judgment of medical students, surgery ranked high but psychiatry ranked lowest in a study by Merton, et al (1956). It is not unexpected then, that women comprise 11.04% of psychiatrists.

Jesse Bernard (1972) has documented the increase in financial rewards and prestige when men take on female occupations, and notes a tendency among young people to shed the old base of prestige. Thus, there are instances of men lawyers now devoting themselves to poverty law, a specialty formerly sex-typed for women lawyers.

It is interesting to note that sex-role differentiation permeates even in the execution of research in the field of sociology. According to Bernard "a masculine bias has been embedded in the structure of inquiry; the most prestigious methods have tended to be those that yielded 'hard' data, and are predominated by men."

The history of sex-typing of occupations changes over time with a concurrent change in the prestige of these occupations. Midwifery was predominantly a female occupation with low prestige, but obstetrics has been, in the United States, a male specialty. Until a few years ago, high school teachers were generally females but as the financial rewards, together with prestige, are on the increase there is a tendency for more men to take up teaching in high schools (Colombotos, 1962; Grimmand Steen, 1974). Clerks used to be predominantly male (and still are in India) but now in the United States, clerical work is almost exclusively a female occupation (Waldman and McEaddy, 1974). Even priesthood is assigned to men and all important ceremonies of birth, death and marriage are performed by men all over the world (except for the Sikh religion in India which allows women to conduct all these ceremonies).

There seems to be an association between the professionalization of an occupation, an increase in financial reward as well as prestige and its being sex-typed as a male occupation. We are not attempting to establish any casual relationships but merely observing a correlation.

## What is the Impact of Sexual Inequity in Medicine?

This sexual inequity in medicine does not give women patients the equal opportunity to select and consult a female doctor if they should so desire. It seems reasonable to assume that women patients should feel more comfortable with a female doctor. Indeed, in one large study conducted by the Kaiser-Permanente Medical Care Program, a clear correlation was observed between the sex of the patient and the sex of the physician when patients were given a free choice (Kelly, 1980).

In another study of undergraduate students, there was preference for a same gender provider and this preference was stronger for all respondents in those services that seemed to be associated with intimacy and physical interaction such as gynecologists, primary physicians and personal counselors (Young, 1979). In one study, college students in the same sex, physician-patient dyads reported more symptom disclosure than patients in opposite sex dyads (Brandenburg, 1981). In view of these findings, it is felt that more women are needed, especially in those specialties which deal with women's diseases. Why are there so few women in female specialties? It is possible that the absence of role models in these specialties, the perception of difficulty of access in residency programs and difficulties in combining family life with specialties like surgery and gynecology (which require a high level of commitment and have unpredictable hours of work) have been barriers to the participation of women in theses areas.

## The Implications of the Increased Number of Women in Medicine and the Observed Change in Specialty Selection.

Would the financial rewards prestige of medicine or certain specialties change in any way with more women in medicine? At this time, with the data examined thus far, it appears that the proportion of women in the medical profession is not large enough to have any significant effect on the prestige of medicine or on the delivery system.

## Effect on the Doctor-Patient Relationship

A patient seeks health care because of a perceived need which is mainly physical in nature, but there is also a strong socio-emotional component which affects the doctor-patient relationship. A satisfactory doctor-patient relationship enhances patient compliance and therefore treatment outcome. With more women in medicine, especially in women's diseases, it is felt that a more satisfactory doctor-patient relationship will result for the female patient.

In a study done on dentists in Manhattan, women felt that men and women patients selected them as dentists because of their gentle touch. Women have their own unique qualities of empathy and support to offer in their encounter with patients. Women caregivers often have shared beliefs and experiences with patients which could provide that additional sensitivity so essential for good patient care.

## The Role of Women in the Care of the Terminal Patient.

Women have always ministered to the care of the sick and dying in the family and in the community. Certain qualities such as caring, empathy, tolerance, patience and selflessness described earlier as feminine traits are ideal characteristics for individuals working with terminal patients and the bereaved. Various surveys demonstrate that patients like doctors who are understanding, show interest, spend enough time, and provide explanations for procedures. Affective qualities are valued more highly than technical or administrative qualities (Segall and Burnett, 1972).

In fact some authors have noted that women doctors tend to spend more time than men doctors with their patients (Cartwritght, 1967) and have a better relationship with the dying patient. It would be interesting to study the impact of the sex of providers of services in reducing the sense of alienation and anomie (loss of control) in hospitalized and terminal patients. Another area for study could be the social mobility of women professionals in the occupational hierarchy of medicine, including the care of terminally-ill patients.

The impact of the sex of providers, on the type and quality of services provided to obstetrics/gynecology patients and terminal patients could be a fruitful area of investigation.

In summing up, most doctors have been men thus far, and most patients express a high level of satisfaction with their doctors. It is not implied anywhere that women should be competing with men. On the contrary, the role of women could have a complementary synergistic effect in the health care delivery system. If patients seek the kind of qualities in their doctors which women doctors demonstrate as discussed here -- then the increase in numbers of women doctors is a very welcome change (Dickinson and Pearson, 1979).

## REFERENCES

American Medical Association. 1979. Physician Distribution and Medical Licensure in the United States. 1977. Chicago: AMA.

American Medical Association. 1981. Physician Characteristics and Distribution in the U.S.: 1981. Monroe: A.M.A.

Bernard, J. 1971. Women and the Public Interest. Chicago: Aldine Pub. Co.

Bernard J. 1973. "My Four Revolutions: An Autobiographical History of the A.S.A." A.J.S. 78(4):784.

Booth, A. 1972. "Sex and Social Participation." A.S.R. 2(37):183-93.

Brandenburg, J.B. 1981. "Gender Preferences for Providers of Health and Counseling Services." J Family Practice 19:289-291.

Cartwright, A. 1967. Patients and Their Doctors: A Study of General Practice. London: Routledge, Keegan Paul.

Colombotos, J.L. 1962. Sources of Professionalism: A Study of High School Teachers. Cooperative Research Project #330. Department of Sociology, University of Michigan, Ann Arbor.

Dahlstrom, E., ed. 1971. The Changing Roles of Men and Women. Boston: Beacon Press.

Dickinson, G.E. and Pearson A.A. 1979. "Sex Differences of Physicians in Relating to Dying Patients." J. American Medical Women's Association 34(1):45-47.

Epstein, C.F. 1970. Woman's Place: Options and Limits in Professional Careers. Berkley: University of California Press.

Galenson, M. 1973. Women and Work: An International Comparison. New York State School of Industrial and Labor Relations. Ithaca: Cornell University Press.

Goswami, M.J. 1978. Women Dentists in Manhattan: A Comparison with Men Dentists. Doctoral dissertation, Graduate School of Arts and Sciences, Columbia University, New York.

Grimm, J.W. and Stern, R.N. 1974. "Sex Roles and Internal Labor Market Structures: The Female Semi-Professionals." Social Problems 21(5):690-705.

Hennig, M. and Jardim, A. 1974. "Behavioral Differences Stressed in Women's Management Training." New York Times, 11 February 1974, 53, 56.

Kehrer, B.H. 1974. Professional and Practice Characteristics of Men and Women Physicians: Profiles of Medical Practice. Chicago: AMA.

Kelly, J.M. 1980. "Sex Preference in Patient Selection of a Family Physician." J of Family Practice, 11(3):427-430.

Kosa, J. and Coker, R.E., Jr. 1965. "The Female Physician in Public Health: Conflict and Reconciliation of the Professional and Sex Roles." Sociology and Social Research 49, p. 295.

Maccoby, E.E. 1963. In S.M. Farber and R.H.L. Wilson, eds. The Potential of Women. New York:McGraw-Hill.

National Academy of Sciences. Annual Summary Reports 1971-1980. "Doctorates Awarded 1920-1971 by Subfield of Doctorate, Sex and Decade," March, 1973; "Doctorate Recipients from United States Universities," Washington, D.C.

National Center for Education Statistics. 1980. Projections of Education Statistics to 1988-89 (NCFS 80-42). Washington, D.C.: U.S. Government Printing Office.

Navarro, V. 1975. "Women in Health Care." New England J of Medicine 292(8):398-402.

Rossi, A.S. 1967. "Barriers to the Career Choice of Engineering, Medicine, or Science Among American Women." In J.A. Matfield and C.G. Van Aken, eds. Women and the Scientific Professions. Cambridge, MA: The MIT Press, pp 113-118.

Segall, A. and Burnett, M. 1980. "Patient Evaluation of Physician Role Performance." Social Science and Medicine 14A:269-278.

Stamm, A.M. 1969. "NASW Membership: Characteristics, Deployment and Salaries." Personnel Information 12:3.

Stanley, R.S. 1971. "The Female in Engineering." In A. Theodore, ed. The Professional Woman. Cambridge, MA: Schenkman Publishing Co. Inc., pp. 398-399.

U.S. Bureau of Labor Statistics. 1979. Employment and Earnings 26(1):172- 173.

U.S. Bureau of the Census. 1975. Statistical Abstract of the United States: 1975. 96th Edition. Washington, D.C.

U.S. Bureau of the Census. 1976. A Statistical Portrait of Women in the U.S. Current Population Reports: Special Studies. Series P-23, No. 58. April 1976.

U.S. Bureau of the Census. 1978. Current Population Reports: Special Studies Series. P-23, No. 113. Selected Characteristics of Persons in the Life Sciences: 1978. P-1A, No. 108. Selected Characteristics of Persons in the Physical Science.

U.S. Bureau of the Census. 1981. Statistical Abstract of the United States: 1981. 102nd Edition. Washington, D.C. p. 108.

U.S. Department of Labor. 1969. Trends in Educational Attainment of Women. (October), p. 10.

Waldman, E. and McEaddy, B.J. 1974. "Where Women Work -- An Analysis of Industry and Occupation." Monthly Labor Review (May) Reprint 2964, pp. 3-13.

Young, W.J. 1979. "Symptom Disclosure to Male and Female Physicians: Effects of Sex, Physical Attractiveness and Symptom Type." Journal of Behavioral Medicine 2(2):159-169.

# THE MEANING OF DEATH AND LOSS FOR WOMEN
## By Don Sloan

Death and loss have special meanings for women. Therefore, it is fitting that obstetricians and gynecologists be called upon to discuss these subjects for they are the primary physicians of women. They are expected to deal with many, if not most, issues concerning how and why women die and how they deal with loss in their lives. Similarly, they are the specialists who treat women for problems of sexual dysfunction. The two are not uncoincidentally linked. How a women is expected to deal with her sexuality is closely related to how she is expected to deal with death.

On the other hand, how fitting is it that we openly discuss so sensitive a matter? How can we speak in public on a topic that strikes fear into any of us, and that we know strikes fear into those for whom we care as healers?

Death is an evil not only because it is final. It is the end of life, and without life, we cannot conceive of functioning in a way that we know to be valid. As Gorki put it in his essay, *On the Good Life*, we spend our valuable energies speculating upon the secrets of death and philosophizing over our investigations into death. Indeed, the human race developed gods and idols to combat its fears, by establishing an "other world" that makes death appear less final than it really is. We prefer those hazy, far-off places we have named "Paradise" and "Hell" to the finality of death. Such creations help fight fear. But, as Gorki also reminded us, death is a phenomenon which demands study for better understanding. Some day, through scientific study, we may achieve the ability, if not to master death, at least to gain better control of it and ourselves. That may be the best we mortals can expect.

Why death? What is its purpose? Why has nature created it? Is this nature's imperfection? We do have something for which to be thankful in death. Death destroys worn-out living beings. Unfortunately, it sometimes destroys life prematurely. It takes youth as well as the aged. It takes the gifted while it leaves us with pedestrian minds. It takes valued and useful animals and leaves us with pests. To understand such phenomena requires better understanding of nature than we already possess.

There are also the deaths that fall under our human control. It is to those forms of death that I now address myself. These are the deaths of people who succumb to the exhaustions of life, to the relentless rape of their energies; the death of those who are born into life so weak that they are barely able to stay alive for a month, the deaths of those whose lives begin with malnutrition and hygiene insufficient to provide what any human being requires to survive so fragile a beginning.

At a recent meeting of the World Health Organization (WHO) in Washington, a group of the world's authorities in maternal and infant care met to exchange ideas for improving their speciality. Most countries were represented. Each member was called upon in turn to describe reasons for his/her own success in decreasing infant and perinatal mortality in his/her nation. A Swiss physician spoke of a new neonatal critical care unit in his hospital. A West German expounded on his hospital's computerized screening of high risk patients. A Californian told of his university's glamorous labor and delivery suite fitted with all the technology grant money could buy. Finally, a Cuban obstetrician took his turn to announce, somewhat simplistically, that he and his colleagues had improved their infant survival and reduced their mortality by providing all of their prenatal patients with shoes. "Shoes?" exclaimed the group in unison. "Shoes," was the reply. The speaker from Havana explained his remark, demonstrating how improvement in the most basic services, matters that are taken for granted by the "developed countries" of the world, can lead directly only not to an obvious improvement in the quality of life, but even to the sustaining of life itself. He pointed out that clean feet and supported arches, and all that means to a person's general health, can improve neonatal recovery.

He drew an analogy for the audience, between the well-being of an otherwise healthy person as the result of simple and persistent toothache, and how the gnawing agony of so localized a pain can lead to a total breakdown. His data showed that prior to the simple improvement he described, one out of five newborns, 20%, died in the first month of life from coliform diarrhea, a rate and incidence of such a disease that would be intolerable among industrial nations. Imagine, there are countries that are striving to develop in such a way that their leading causes of death may be from highway accidents and heart attacks; causes which stand as hallmarks of industrial and intellectual development.

Is it not the rigor of such an over-mechanized life style that exhausts us? Do we not become fatigued by the sapping of our energies? Which members of our society fulfill their expected life span, and which die too early? To whom is life precious and to whom is it less valuable? As time goes on, we become more advanced, and life becomes more protected. Yet we are also taught, somehow, that there are those among us for whom life is expendable. Can that be true?

The burdens of sexism which cross all class barriers have especially caused women to pay a dear price for whatever rewards they may gain from society. Women have too long functioned as an underprivileged group. Men have also too long paid the price of sexism, by feeling compelled to work to provide for two instead of one. The mechanics of that decaying system and its meanings are beyond the scope and intent of this chapter.

What we should consider here is how we, as physicians, have approached this situation. How well equipped are we, as obstetricians/gynecologists, to deal with the problems of our female patients and their need to face the death of a loved one or their own deaths? It seems to me that we have not accomplished this adequately. I recall no training at all in these matters, during my medical education. You might even say the issue was ignored, or approached in a pejorative manner.

My teachers practiced the stereotyping of the female on many levels including impending death, and after death had occurred. One highly regarded physician was required to explain the need for surgery on an ovarian cyst, to a loyal patient who had great respect for him. She expressed her anxieties about her impending surgery and anesthesia; especially her underlying fear of dying from either. She acknowledged that rationally she had to overcome her emotions, because she accepted the need for the operation.

As their conversation progressed, this doctor lost the patient and her respect. In his effort to soothe her anxiety, he said that, while it was true that she had the cyst, and needed the surgery, but she should be able to see the silver lining in the cloud. There was a good chance, he urged, that the cyst might be benign -- most were. She realized, then, that he fully expected that this response would enable her to relax and relieve her of her stress, and that her fears of dying should be banished from her thoughts.

As she later discussed her feelings with me, she described how her attitude towards the surgeon had changed. "What," she wondered, "would he have said if it had been a male patient, with a prostatic tumor?" She challenged whether a male patient would have been dismissed with the implication that hope for non-malignancy should be enough to eliminate the fear of death. Was this, I wondered, an example of how my gynecologic colleagues approach their patients; reducing their obligations to deal with death to patronizing platitudes? Are our women patients regarded as insufficiently strong to handle honesty?

When physicians say, "Let me speak to your husband," are they expressing the same attitude as when they say, "Let me speak to your wife?" Do they ever say the latter? Do we encounter death in men with one attitude and in women with another? Do we consider that the economic warrior and wage earner deserves to be dealt with on a superior level; while women, are relegated to the Freudian-Deutschian role of narcissists, masochists, and non-aggressors, and are therefore to be dealt with on a less mature level? Can it be that the death of a male signifies the loss of a wage-earner while the death of a woman requires replacing "only" a child-raiser or home-maker?

Are such social assignments deserved? I think not. For although women's freedom and equality will be truly won when women achieve economic freedom and equality, their power to deal with death has been clearly demonstrated over the centuries. As a group, compared to men, women are less fearful of death because they have been allowed to feel more. Although sexism calls it a weakness, to feel is actually a strength. As men permit themselves to feel more of their emotions and express them, they, too, will gain the rewards of such strength.

# RADIATION THERAPY AND GYNECOLOGIC CANCERS
## By Richard Torpie

Radiation oncology enters the treatment of gynecologic cancers in approximately 60% of all cancers of the ovary, uterus, cervix, and vagina. The good results generally obtained by prompt treatment of early stage cancers is the result of excellent collaboration between the gynecologist and the radiation oncologist, and more recently, the medical oncologist. Radiation therapy, however, is not the type of medical specialty that is regarded in a positive light. Often the radiation therapy facility of a hospital is relegated to a bleak sub-basement, somewhere near the laundry and the incinerator. The hallways in which patients congregate are frequently located on the lobbies of the medical floors, and the radiation oncologist is often located out of that mainstream. Not only do we have a problem with the professional perception of our work, but also the lay perception is distorted.

People are referred to radiation therapy centers for various reasons. The reaction, however, of most patients who are referred to high dose radiation is one of dismay, a response to the recognition that their condition is more serious than they had imagined. Often the information provided, preceding such referrals has been insufficient or the patient has been misinformed. Sufficient misinformation may interfere with the patient's response even to the most beneficial therapy.

The majority of patients who are treated with radiation, either with cobalt or high external beams, are usually exposed daily for a period of four to seven weeks. Not only the principal location of the tumor, but also the surrounding area encompassing lymph nodes, or other areas of known probable metastatic disease are exposed. The treatments themselves are no more painful than a chest X-ray. Resulting side effects or injuries from radiation therapy are cumulative. Often when the pelvic region is treated, symptoms commonly appear which may be controlled by diet and medication. Other reactions may include redness of skin, permanent or at least sub-acute, loss of pubic hair, irritation of the bladder lining, and often vaginal irritation. Severe, life-threatening complications can occur, usually in periods following radiation therapy. At a reputable center, such major complications are probably limited to about 5% of the patients. These may include rectal, or bladder necrosis, and damage to the small intestine. In most cases, these are treated by surgical rescue and rarely cause death.

I first studied gynecologic oncology at Heinemann Medical College, which at the time, saw more gynecologic tumors than all the other institutions in Southeastern Pennsylvania, Southern New Jersey, and Delaware, combined. In one year, we treated over 350 major gynecologic tumors. Thus certain phenomena struck me in my formative years, making permanent impressions.

First, when women were seen in consultation, only in rare circumstances was a male figure -- husband or lover -- present. Second, while death prevention measures were discussed, such "secondary" issues as body image, loss of femininity, loss of sexuality, future rehabilitative use of sexual organs, loss of reproduction, or loss of hormonal function of the ovaries were generally overlooked. In every case, radiation therapy in the premenopausal or paramenopausal woman will cause sterility. Interestingly, until recent years, I have rarely seen sterility noted as a side effect, or complication on a permission-to-treat form. This situation may reflect the fact that most radiation oncologists are men, who are not sensitive to such a significant loss.

Approximately one-fourth of patients who are treated with radiation may, at some point in their treatment, be exposed to radium or other concentrated radiation isotopes. This treatment usually occurs most commonly under anaesthesia. This procedure involves a great deal of loss of modesty; often some distortion of a placement of a patient are involved with measurement, with pre-placement of the isotope, with removal of the radium device.

Also, a certain sense of isolation occurs, since the patient is placed in a room by herself. No matter how much we try to manage otherwise, a certain avoidance is manifested by the nursing staff; nobody wants exposure to excess radiation, although this risk has been shown to be minimal when measured in the nursing staff. Often the patient reacts to this as an "assault" on her body, not only on the cancer. The treatment seems threatening, as administered by a huge, mysterious radiation device. Once I tried lying on the table to see how it looked, and it <u>was</u> frightening: here are these sterile, chromium-like mechanical devices, with some mysterious element, are inserted within the vagina, or within the cervix, or the uterus, producing fears of burning, and other dire effects. Examinations, of course, are usually pelvic, and must be carried out vigorously to determine the tumor response. These examinations occur continuously over the course of therapy and the follow-up examinations.

I've been impressed by the fact that the majority of women who we see are fully informed about their bodies and about the potential of their cancers. But in many cases involving radical or definitive surgery, accompanied by definitive or even radical radiation therapy, we encounter patients who are poorly informed regarding the loss of function, or the limited amount of rehabilitation that may occur, and also in whom the expected losses of body function are not addressed. We discuss sterility, but we seldom mention disruption of the menstrual cycle, premature menopause in younger women, change of hormonal function. Feminist writers have presented the issues, but have done little to provide solutions which are workable within the framework of an oncology service.

The issue of guilt is also connected with cancer. This disease, in some cultures, evokes a sense of sin, or retribution for sin. It also involves shame, especially since the situation requires a "stranger" to examine a woman's pelvis. Such shame leads to delay in treatment.

The association of guilt, sin and cancer suggests that cancer has replaced leprosy and tuberculosis as the pariah's disease of our society. Patients fear loss of control, fear the unknown, fear recurrence, fear death. The radiation oncologist, who may be uncomfortable with women, represents the <u>science</u> of medicine, as contrasted to the comfortable <u>art</u> of medicine. Often he fails to enlist cooperation; approximately 5% of patients who start radiation therapy, even in a supportive facility, fail to complete the possibly curative course. Sexual rehabilitation, particularly important for patients who may have tired of their cancer, is poorly addressed, and often blocked by the patient or family. Again, we usually see little involvement of the male figure in this kind of situation.

In cases of advanced cancer, where modes of treatment are often experimental and challenging, greater stress is exerted upon the patient by the family. Such situations create a greater sense of frustration and arouse preconceived notions regarding the possible success of therapy. The challenge both to the medical oncologist and the radiation oncologist is that once we reach absolutes of cure, the next step for a greater cure must involve accepting the discomfort of protocols, of drugs which may be experimental and minimally successful. But only through such means, and the courage of our patients, will advances in medicine be achieved.

Protocols are considered oppressive in situations involving lack of support. We do see small miracles in ovarian cancer, (thanks to newer drugs, newer methods of availability). One patient recently entered into the underground network of cancer cures from Boston to Evanston, Illinois and other places and another basically reviewed 8 months later demonstrated that society's sense. For example, tumor and liver cancers are beyond the scope of radiation therapy. We began a program of experimental chemotherapy. By the time she was reviewed, she was free of any evidence of cancer.

The fantasy held by patients with regard to their cancer can often take on some former desire. It's not uncommon for women with ovarian cancer to fantasize pregnancy as an analogy to their situation. The bloating, the swelling of the abdomen, the actual presence of mass, in a way, can mimic pregnancy and often women have talked to me of their need to deliver their tumor. When cancer becomes incurable, and grows in the pelvis, interfering with rectal and urinary function, the patient faces one of the most distressing problems in medicine in terms of pain and of meaningful nursing care. It requires great courage for the terminal patient in such a situation, to keep dignity and life together. Very few cures, potential cures, or treatments of cancer can match the agonizing distress of severe cancer for which treatment has failed.

We must think strongly of alternatives of strong support, not only for patients in a terminal situation, but also for cancer patients who may yet become terminal. Support must start at Day One of diagnosis, and continue throughout all levels of patient care, whether the end is cure or eventual death. Involvement of family and loved ones at all levels of care is paramount. The reintroduction of the absent male figure into the life of the patient may end what may be considered a "porcelain-doll syndrome," in which the patient is treated like somebody who will break, becoming further isolated from family interactions. Potential feelings of guilt or shame regarding the cancer may be reinforced by social isolation from friends and even from the caregiver. It is reasonable to expect a degree of regression in the dying person which involves the need to foster a trust. With this trust arises a need to have the caregivers assume, in a sense, a primitive mothering role, whereby pain and suffering of these patients may be minimized. Such a function is altogether possible when concepts such as thanatology and hospice are utilized skillfully, and with concern and care by a staff which is supported in every respect.

The patient must learn to participate in all the care-providing decisions that affect her. Too often, women have been isolated as if, by some decree, they have lost control over their lives and destinies. Certainly, a sufficient militancy of spirit is indicated on the part of the patient to guarantee that her care is appropriate, that all options have been explored, and that all considerations regarding her future, her prognosis, and the eventuality of a terminal situation, have been fully considered. This awareness also includes attention to finances, at a time when everybody is squeezing the medical budget. We must resist shrinking from the potential costs of supporting patients with terminal cancer, supplying appropriate hospitalizations and hospice care with government or third party payment.

The issues here are multiple. One of the first patients I treated at St. Luke's Hospital had advanced ovarian cancer with disseminated abdominal, thoracic, and a large cerebral neck mass. I apologized profusely because we were not properly organized and the orderly had brought this lady downstairs when she should have been left in bed. My own instinct with this patient would have been, however not to treat. She looked at me and said, "What are you waiting for? I'm not down here for the ride; start doing something." I did begin her treatment.

The tumor did melt away. We switched from the abdomen to the chest, into the neck; the tumor here melted away, with surprisingly low doses of radiation. She eventually died two years later, of her cancer. However, few people have impressed me as much as she did, by the good measure of life she led during that period. It is an injustice to patients who are dying, to deny them good medical care because of some fantasy that the treatment may be worse than the cure, or than the disease. I think radiation is important, if only to relieve pain, by offering some alleviation to the oppressive onset and eventual progress of disease. Sometimes the disease is diverted by attempts to cure, so that even if the cure fails, the patient gets some time and comfort. The radiation oncologist, as the medical oncologist, probably deals with cancer more often than any other specialist. He needs the support of patients educated to understand the problems that they are facing, and who can function in a partnership with empathy and knowledge.

# UTILIZING HEALTH INFORMATION AFTER THE DIAGNOSES OF BREAST CANCER:
# A HEALTH EDUCATION PROGRAM MODEL
### Rose M. Savage Jackman

Providing health information to the public is vital in disease prevention and health promotion. Programs designed to promote changes in behavior and to encourage regular doctor visits have become an essential task of health educators. When the public is more knowledgeable about health practices, there is a reduction in illness and disease.

Written materials to support that goal can be found in doctors' offices and patient lounges, describing the causes of disease and ways to help prevent them. Some of the publications may have a section on how disease is treated. What is not usually found is information on what to do if one is diagnosed with a major illness. When this occurs, patients must rapidly digest information about the terminology and process for cure to make the medical decisions that will affect their health, employment, family, and emotions. Such is the case when breast cancer is diagnosed.

Breast cancer is the most commonly diagnosed type of cancer and the second leading cause of cancer death among women in the United States. It is estimated that 182,000 will be diagnosed with breast cancer in the United States in 1994. The breast cancer incidence rate for women has increased about 2% a year since 1980. Most of that increase is believed to be due to greater utilization of mammography, allowing earlier detection of the disease. Other reasons for rate increases are not yet understood. Although incidence rates have increased, early detection and improved treatment has kept mortality rates fairly stable over the past 50 years.

The projections for 1995 forecast 185,640 new cases in this country and of those, New York will contribute 15,000 new cases. (Cancer Facts & Figures, 1994)

Devastation is the first reaction to news of a breast cancer diagnosis. It is reported that "women only hear about ten percent of what is being said to them at the time of diagnoses" (McGinn, Halock, 1994). Although responses vary, the general message when told "you have cancer" is the belief that you are going to die. Dr. Audrey Lorde, a cancer survivor and well regarded educator and poet, wrote in her <u>The Cancer Journals</u>, the following:

> Each woman responds to the crisis that breast cancer brings to her life out of a whole pattern, which is the design of who she is and how her life has been lived. I do not wish my anger and pain and fear about cancer to fossilize into yet another silence, nor to rob me of whatever strength can lie at the core of this experience, openly acknowledged and examined. Breast cancer is not a unique experience, but

one shared by thousands of American women. Each one of us struggles daily with the pressures of conformity and the loneliness of differences from which those choices seem to offer escape. I only know that those choices do not work for me, nor for other women who, not without fear, have survived cancer by scrutinizing its meaning within our lives, and by attempting to integrate this crisis into useful strengths for change. (1980)

An important aspect of health educators' tasks is providing patients with the information that will help them in the decision-making process. With so much controversy about causes, and so many published defenses of each theory, women find it difficult to obtain definitive answers about the choices they must make to help them decide on treatment. Unlike other illnesses, where medical consensus has been reached, there is none in early-stage breast cancer.

Yet patient participation in medical decision-making has not only become more common but has also become mandatory by legislation. New York State has passed a statute requiring the disclosure of treatment alternatives, enacted in 1985 (N.Y. Public Health Law 2404). Other states also have passed similar rulings. In New York, the law directs the physician to give a written summary of alternatives to the patient.

The source for information given to patients in New York state is a booklet published by the State Health Department, "Breast Cancer." The booklet covers diagnosis, surgery, reconstruction, radiation, chemo- and hormonal therapy, support groups, a glossary, additional resources, and organizations to call. In spite of the legislative ruling, it is not known how many breast cancer patients are given this information and moreover, how effective this information is.

Although many patients are informed at the time of diagnosis that they may have to go through a series of treatments, each time a new process is undertaken, they have to start again, studying the treatment's benefits and risks. They are faced with making choices about different kinds of surgery, breast reconstruction, and hormone therapy as well as tomoxifen.

In a study carried out at the University of Michigan, 48 early-stage women were interviewed while they were in the process of making a decision. Patients related their experiences in forming a judgement. Based on their responses, they were either defined by the scholars as "considered deferrers" (immediate action to one option), "delayers" (considering at least 2 options) or "deliberators" (considering and decomposing at least 2 options). Although no definitive conclusions could be derived from this sample size (n=48), it was concluded that "each decision-making style has unique characteristics that suggest the need for more individualized interventions and support for patients making difficult decisions" (Pierce, 1993).

There are many factors women take into account when deciding about breast cancer treatment. A study by Ward, Heidrich, and Wolberg, "Factors Women Take Into Account When Deciding on Type of Surgery for Breast Cancer," showed that a majority of women prefer active participation in initial decision-making. An important source of information consistently identified was "people" sources. As many as half of the respondents required 'shared' decision-making with a spouse or friend closely involved in the process.

Of this group, 85% felt they wanted to make this decision with their physician, 41% with their families, and with friends, 36%. This study also concluded that women paid very little attention to clinic handouts, videos, and scientific journals. The authors found that providing information in a format of standardized summaries may not be consistent with the preference or needs of a majority of patients. (1989)

The role of information provided to patients faced with decision-making was examined by Katherine Hughes in an exploratory study. She researched the relationship between information about breast cancer, treatment alternatives, and patient choices of treatment. One finding was that a patient's recall of information conveyed around the time of diagnosis is exceedingly poor. The subjects' choice of treatment was unrelated to the amount of information they received or its presentation. Information provided by professionals, relatives, friends, or brochures did not affect treatment choices. "What did affect patients' choices was the information received early from their physician, family, and friends." (1993)

<u>A sampling of newly diagnosed breast cancer patients.</u>

As a graduate student in Community Health Education and a cancer patient, I felt it was important to discover how women actually utilize information they acquire. More important, with so much available did women sense this overload as a problem in understanding treatment options? I developed a questionnaire and presented it to ten women who had been newly diagnosed, to discuss their experiences in using information for deciding on treatment.

Those questioned were:

a) participants in the Brooklyn SHARE Restoration Group,
b) a cancer survivor from Long Island College Hospital in Brooklyn, New York, and
c) cancer survivors who work at State University of New York Health Science Center at Brooklyn.

All the women had either made or were in the process of making treatment choices. The interviews were conducted over the telephone in November, 1994.

Of the ten participants one had been diagnosed in the past three months, five in the past six months, and four in the past year. These figures indicate that the majority had already made several treatment choices and had experiences in gathering information for treatment decisions. They were asked what occurred at the time of diagnosis, how they obtained information about treatment, and how they comprehended it.

Many of them felt that the timing and setting of the disclosure of the diagnosis was most important. While it is understood that there is no easy way to inform anyone they have the disease, not one woman in the study felt that their physicians had properly communicated this frightening news at the right time or in the right place. One woman said:

> I was on the operating table and was told that I had cancer. He [the surgeon] then went on to ask me if I wanted a mastectomy or lumpectomy. I told him, "Neither, I want my husband."

Although this woman remembers being told that she might have to make a choice based on the outcome of the biopsy, she did not want to make that choice on an operating table. This manner of informing patients may occur because surgeons get immediate results from the laboratory about the tumor during an exploratory operation, and hesitate to bring women back to the operating room several times. Although this method may expedite treatment, it distresses patients and does not adhere to the legal statutes concerning disclosure and informed consent.

Almost all the women I spoke with said that while they received either written information or spoke to the physician about treatment, they preferred the physician to make the surgical choice between mastectomy or lumpectomy.

> The doctor should not leave it up to you to make a decision. He should make it for you.

> ...they [doctors] should be trained to be more sensitive to patients and help you understand more about the treatment choices. When he [the doctor] asked me [what my choice was, I said], 'I don't know what to do.'

It is obvious that no one wants to make inappropriate decisions about treatment. The majority of these women did not want the responsibility of sorting through medical or pathological information. Many finally came to a decision by letting the physician choose what the best treatment for them was -- only a few made a choice about which procedure they wanted the doctor to do.

All of the women I spoke to had undergone surgery as their initial cancer treatment. I asked them where they obtained information about other treatments after surgery. Their responses indicated that often they were referred to an oncologist post-operatively, who selected the type of chemotherapy. They were not given a set of choices to explore. At the time of the oncology visit, women were often given a list discussing the side effects of chemotherapy and explanations of the need for a balanced and healthy diet.

They revealed that information about cancer treatment was located in several places. Some was given to patients by a nurse or physician; some was found by calling 1-800-4-CANCER, or by reading it in a book. Some information was obtained from family, friends, or other cancer survivors. But the one thing that emerged was that the information could not be found in one place. Further, no one really knew how to go about putting all this information together to make a decision.

An important aspect of this survey was to determine if information received by the cancer survivor was comprehensible. Each woman was asked to describe the information as "very easy," "easy," or "difficult to understand." In general, they felt that information received from the physician's office and from cancer agencies was easy to understand. When asked the question, "of the information you received, which did you find the most helpful?" all considered information received from other cancer survivors to be the most helpful. Some of their comments about what was most useful in decision-making were:

> I survived breast cancer because of women who had survived breast cancer before me. Those things that my doctor told me that I did not understand I told to my SHARE member, and then I was able to understand.

> Talking about it with another cancer survivor made me see clearly the whole process for going through cancer. She took time to explain things to me. Just hearing women in my group, I could now remember what I heard the doctor tell me. And some things I read but did not quite understand, other women made clear to me.

The final part of this survey was aimed at eliciting opinions on improving information about treatment and access to that information. One of the suggestions was:

> It's (information) spread out all over. The best thing for a doctor to do is to have all the information in one place so you don't have to go to different places looking for it.

## Summary

The information gathered from women participating in this project suggests that cancer patients prefer that the news be given at a more appropriate place and time. Information given to women from the doctor or nurse about surgical options was easy to understand. But women rated the information from cancer survivors as the best source for information. Although there is much information available for women diagnosed with cancer, this information is spread out between too many different agencies and locations.

## A HEALTH EDUCATION PROGRAM MODEL

The findings of this survey indicate that a model comprehensive health education program for women who must face treatment choices should be created. This model would not try to replace the splendid programs that are in place; rather it aims to consolidate the information from these agencies in one location.

An excellent model for health education exists at Harlem Hospital in New York City, headed by Dr. Harold Freeman, a renowned breast surgeon who developed the Cancer Control Center of Harlem (CCCH). CCCH serves as a resource center for the Harlem community. One aspect of the program is the navigation which focuses on the patient's needs to insure prompt follow-up and thorough patient care. Patients are identified immediately and are given information by a cancer specialist who counsels the patient through the treatment process. They are provided other assistance such as help with health insurance and follow-up care. In other medical settings, surgical nurses perform the task of patient follow-up care after the diagnosis of cancer. Patient tracking is also done at major cancer centers such as Memorial Sloane-Kettering Hospital in New York City.

How does one go about developing a health program when financial resources are diminishing? Where would we get the funding for training personnel, medical consultants and written material? The unique aspect of this concept is that we do not have to "reinvent the wheel." The information for a comprehensive program is already in place but it needs to be consolidated. Free and available literature from the National Cancer Institute (NCI), obtained from its Physician Data Base, could be offered as the reading material. NCI also provides fact sheets and abstracts from the Cancerlit database, and disseminated through a service called CancerFax. NCI's materials would be consolidated into one packet, updated regularly, and divided into four categories as follows:

1) Terms used to describe breast cancer
2) Questions for the patient to ask the doctor
3) Suggested reading lists and where to obtain the publications
4) Resources and referrals in the local area.

Since most hospitals have cancer support services, they could develop a team which would provide patient services for assisting with the decision-making process.

## CONCLUSION

Health information is essential to the health of a nation. With so many new and effective methods of treating illness, it is essential that we provide information for patients grappling with the decision-making process. The most effective way for patients to receive and understand treatment is from other patients. A comprehensive program for women seems necessary. The cost for such a service does not have to affect the budget within the health care system. Rather, with the dedication of medical providers, volunteers and survivors, information about breast cancer can be made available to help with the process of recovery.

To assess the need for such a program would require further studies using larger samples, both of newly-diagnosed patients, and physicians who treat breast cancer.

---

### BREAST CANCER INFORMATION QUESTIONNAIRE

My name is Rose Jackman, and I am a graduate student at Hunter College School of Health Sciences. I am also a breast cancer survivor. As part of a class assignment, I am asking women who have been diagnosed with breast cancer to tell me about their experiences in learning about the disease and available treatment. I will also ask questions about support you received and from whom, and about your feelings since you have recovered from cancer.

The information you give will be kept confidential and will be used to help develop an informational brochure for other women who have survived breast cancer. The Interview should take approximately 15 minutes.

November 1994                                             Respondent No._____

---

1. There are several ways that women may discover problems with their breast. How did you first find out there were problems with your breast? Was it . . .
   
   YES    NO
   
   a. through self breast exam
   b. results of a mammogram

c. during a routine doctor's visit
   d. you noticed changes in your breast
   e. any other way_____

2. How long ago were you diagnosed with breast cancer?

   a. in the past three months
   b. in the past six months
   c. in the past nine months
   d. in the past year (since October, 1993)
   e. more than a year ago (before October, 1993)

3. When you were told that you had breast cancer what did the doctor say to you?
   _____
   _____

4. Have you been treated or completed treatment for breast cancer
   YES    Go to Question 4a
   NO     Go to Question 5

4a. Which treatments have you already had . . .

   lumpectomy
   mastectomy
   radiation
   chemotherapy
   hormone therapy
   other treatment_____

5. I am going to ask you some questions about how you obtained information about treatment for breast cancer. This information could have been obtained by explanation or by written material. Tell me, did you obtain information about treatment..
                              YES    NO
   a. from a doctor or a nurse
   b. material on tables in a doctor's office
   c. from a friend
   d. from another breast cancer survivor
   e. from an organization you called about treatment
   f. from the library or bookstore
   g. from television programs
   h. any other way_____

5a. For each yes response in Question 5, Ask:

You said that you obtained information from (NAME). Was the information difficult, easy or very easy to understand?
DIFFICULT   EASY   VERY EASY
   a. from a doctor or a nurse
   b. material on tables in a doctor's office
   c. from a friend
   d. from another breast cancer survivor
   e. from an organization you called about treatment
   f. from the library or bookstore
   g. any any other way

6. Now that we have survived breast cancer, many people helped us through this difficult time. Examine the following list, and please tell me if any of these people gave you any kind of support during these times.
YES   NO   N/A
   a. parents
   b. spouse or lover
   c. family members
   d. medical persons
   e. co workers or people at work
   f. clergy or members at church
   g. other breast cancer survivor
   h. any one else_____

7. Did you receive any kind of support from an organization?

   Yes     Go to Question 7A
   No      Go to Question 8

7a. What are the names of the organizations? _____
_____

7b. How did the organization(s) help you?
_____
_____
_____
_____

8. In addition to organizations, people are often referred to other places for followup care (during/after) treatment. Were you referred to any of the following places? For each yes answer, ask: Did you attend . . .

                        YES                NO              ATTEND

    a. self help groups
    b. a nutritionist or dietician
    c. another doctor other than oncologist
    d. cosmetologist
    e. hairstylist
    f. any other group_____

9. In what ways can organizations better help women who have been diagnosed with breast cancer?

_____
_____
_____
_____

10. I am interested in what you think about some issues. I would like to know if you strongly agree, agree, disagree, strongly disagree or are undecided about:

                                  SA  A  DA  SD  U

    a. The government is doing all it can to cure breast cancer.
    b. In general, medical personnel are able to communicate information about breast cancer well?
    c. Information regarding breast cancer is accessible to women in my community.

11. Please tell me if the following is true or false.

                                TRUE          FALSE

    a. My health insurance covered all of my medical expenses.
    b. My job was not affected because of my illness.
    c. My relationship with my family is better now.
    d. I am more aware of my health now.
    e. I was taught how to do a self breast exam.
    f. I keep all of my doctor appointments.
    g. I am helping other breast cancer survivors.
    h. I have changed my diet.
    i. I am making plans for the future.

# REFERENCES

American Cancer Society, Cancer Facts and Figures, 1994, Atlanta: American Cancer Society, 1994: Publication #5008.

Dow, Karen Hassey. New Developments in the Diagnosis and Staging of Breast Cancer. Seminars in Oncology Nursing. Vol 7 No. 7, pp. 156-174. August 1991.

Hughes, Katharine Kostbade. Decision-Making by Patients with Breast Cancer: The Role of Information in Treatment Selection. Oncology Nursing Forum, Vol. 20, No. 4, pp. 623-628, 1993.

Kelsey, J.L. Breast Cancer Epidemiology: Summary and Future Direction. Epidemiology Review, 15. pp. 256-63, 1993.

Lerman Caryn, Daly Mary, Walsh, Resch, Nancy, et al. Communication Between Patients with Breast Cancer and Health Care Providers and Implications. Cancer, Vol. 72, No. 9, pp. 2612-2619. November 1, 1993.

Lorde, Audrey. The Cancer Journals. Argyle: Spinsters, Ink, 1980.

Centers for Disease Control and Prevention. Mortality, Morbidity Weekly Report. U.S. Dept. of Health & Human Services. Vol. 43 no. 15, pp. 273-281 April 22, 1994

Nayfield, Susan G., Bongiovanni, Gregory C., Alciati, Marianne H, et al. Statutory Requirements for Disclosure of Breast Cancer Treatment Alternatives. Journal of the National Cancer Institute, Vol. 86, No. 16, pp. 1202-1208, August 17, 1994.

Osteen, R.T., Karnell, L.H. The National Cancer Data Base Report on Breast Cancer. Cancer. 73(7): 1994-2000, 1994

Pierce, Penny F. Deciding on Breast Cancer Treatment: A Description of Decision-Making Behavior. Nursing Research Jan/Feb,42: 22-28, 1993.

Tanne, Janice Hopkins. Everything You Need to Know about Breast Cancer...But Were Afraid to Ask. New York. Ladies Home Journal, 53-62. October 11, 1993.

Roberts, Gloria S., Cox, Charles, E., Reintgen, Douglas, S., et al. Influence of Physician Communication on Newly Diagnosed Breast Patient's Psychological Adjustment and Decision-Making. Cancer Supplement, Vol 74, No, 1, pp. 336-341. July 1, 1994,

Ward S. Heidrich S. Wolberg W.: Factors women take into account when deciding upon type of surgery for breast cancer. Cancer Nursing, 12:344-351, 1989

COPING WITH AIDS IN AN INNER-CITY POPULATION
Chantal Bruchez-Hall, PhD, Nanette Nelson, PhD,
and Anita Sussman, MSW

## HIV/AIDS: THE EPIDEMIC

In June, 1981, the Centers for Disease Control in Atlanta reported the first case of a disease that would claim thousands of American lives within a decade. The acronyms "HIV" and "AIDS," "human immunodeficiency virus" and "acquired immuno-deficiency syndrome," were virtually unknown but are now recognized as a virtual death sentence.

Knowledge about prevention of AIDS has not been spread rapidly enough to prevent at least 249,199 adults and 4,249 children in the United States from developing AIDS by December 1992. Of these reported cases, 171,890 have died (Centers for Disease Control, 1993). Although more males than females are infected each year, the rate of AIDS cases in women has increased alarmingly. Of the 11,987 women newly diagnosed in 1991 and 1992, 5,635 (47%) were IV drug users, and 4,622 (38.6%) were infected through heterosexual contact. During the same period, 1,463 cases of pediatric AIDS have been reported; 518 (35.4%) of their mothers had used IV drugs, and 433 (29.5%) were infected through heterosexual contact (222 or 15% of this latter group had fathers who used IV drugs).

Estimates of the total number of people who test positive for HIV range from two to ten times the reported number of AIDS cases. Therefore between 24,000 and 120,000 women and between 3,000 and 15,000 children were estimated to be HIV-infected as of December 1992.

## WOMEN, CHILDREN AND THE FAMILY

With so many women and children affected by the disease, the burden of caring for the survivors falls upon families and society. Traditionally, women assume the major role in handling the social and emotional tasks of bereavement, from the expression of grief to the care of surviving family members, while men are often prohibited from expressing their grief by their upbringing. This may be especially true in poor, inner-city neighborhoods. Therefore, while the pain of loss is not limited to females, the focus of this article is upon the unique experience of women who are victims of this epidemic. Special attention will be paid to the issues faced by the caregivers of children who have acquired the disease at birth and the difficult decisions that must be made.

One cannot address the issue of women and AIDS without being forced to deal with questions of reproductive decisions and pediatric AIDS. As most women infected with HIV/AIDS are in their reproductive years, they have or may have children. Reproduction is one of the most acute issues faced by HIV-infected women since most newborns will be orphaned and 20% to 35% of the children perinatally exposed to HIV will remain infected.

It is estimated that more than 80,000 children will be orphaned by the year 2000 (Michaels & Levine, 1992). A woman is frequently diagnosed as HIV-positive when she seeks obstetrical care. External pressures from her partner, friends, and family to terminate or maintain the pregnancy may be severe and contradictory. When care is sought during the period that abortion is an ethical alternative, the mother should be assisted in exploring her medical options as well as her own values and goals before a decision is made to continue the pregnancy.

When an HIV-positive woman gives birth, it is not inevitable that the child will also be HIV-positive. There is a period of several months after birth when the ultimate status of the child may be unknown. When blood tests confirm that the child is HIV negative, the mother's decision to bear the child is ratified. When the baby is infected, she must not only face her own illness and death, but confront all the issues that parents face when a child is diagnosed with a terminal illness. Furthermore, the HIV-positive mother, who urgently needs to protect her own health by minimizing stress and obtaining adequate rest and nutrition, will most likely deplete her energy caring for the infected child.

Frequently a child is the first member of the family diagnosed with HIV, triggering the diagnosis of the mother and/or father and sometimes one or more siblings (Needle, Leach, Graham-Tomasi, 1989). This is the worst possible scenario; the entire family may be dying and no one had early warning. In recent memory, only war has decimated families in this manner. Treatment of the disease does not fit the traditional medical model since the infected as well as the uninfected family members become the patients. Ideally, arrangements for medical care and education regarding the course of the disease and prevention of opportunistic infections would include all those involved in the care of infected family members. Legal issues such as guardianship of surviving children and disposal of property would also be arranged while the parents are physically able to do so.

Patients can live normal lives for more than 10 years, others deteriorate and die quickly. Most likely there will be periods of crisis in which patients will need a great deal of care and support followed by remissions during which they will function independently and well. New treatment regimens provide hope for improved quality of life and length of survival, but may also have negative side effects and prove detrimental. The entire family may require counseling to assist them in dealing with the emotional highs and lows as well as the social pressures associated with living with HIV/AIDS. Once a family has found a source of medical care, access to ancillary services such as financial aid, counseling, physical therapy, and early intervention for children, is usually facilitated. Depending on the number of family members requiring services, keeping appointments may become a full time job for the patient and/or other caretakers. During periods of remission, this schedule may prove beneficial, providing not only the intended services but a source of social support from professionals as well as other patients and families who are living with AIDS. In times of crisis, it may be overwhelmingly difficult (Needle, et al., Tiblier, et al.).

## COMPLEX ISSUES OF BEREAVEMENT AND MULTIPLE LOSS

All the issues faced by a family when a child is dying are multiplied in this epidemic. It is impossible to predict how any one family will adapt and cope with the grief inherent in this subject. One can only discuss how, in theory, individuals deal with loss and suggest how recovery may evolve once the ordeal of the family is over. HIV/AIDS is an implied death sentence, but it is also a chronic illness. Once the initial shock has passed, parents generally become busy with the practical matters discussed above, especially with arrangements for treatment of the disease (Kupst, 1986). While the patient appears healthy there is concern and fear, but life is fairly routine until the first crisis. At this point the reality of the threat of AIDS can no longer be denied and family members may experience anticipatory grief for the first time.

Anticipatory grief is not simply the psychological and/or somatic response to the loss of a loved one that begins prior to the actual death. It is a multidimensional concept that exists from two perspectives, that of the patient and that of the family. In this case "family" also encompasses friends, caretakers and all others who are concerned with the welfare of the patient. Anticipatory grief focuses on three periods of time: past, present, and future (Rando, 1986). The grief is not only for the loss of the person that will die at some point in the future, but for the loss of the vital person one knew in the past, and for the one currently dying. There is also a complex interaction of psychological, social, and physiological factors that influence anticipatory grief. They include, among other things, the meaning and nature of the relationship between the griever and the patient, the unfinished business they may share, their personal characteristics and coping abilities, and past experiences with illness, death and dying. Anticipatory mourning can be therapeutic, allowing gradual adjustment to the impending loss for all parties.

The anticipatory grief of the patient entails the recognition that life, as she has known it, is now limited. All previous goals, values and beliefs must be reevaluated. Unresolved problems, coping with the loss of loved ones as well as one's self, anticipation of future pain, and loss of abilities must be faced. For the mother of an AIDS-infected child, her personal death and the adjustment to it may be complicated by guilt, anger, and the need to accept the fact that she will possibly see her child deteriorate and die before she does.

There is some evidence that there is "an optimum amount of anticipatory grief" but, in periods of illness that are too long or too short, the survivors may be prone to abnormal grief following the death. The ideal amount of preparation serves ". . . to bring people together and to heighten emotional attachment, too much of it or inappropriate application of its processes can result in premature detachment from the dying person" (Rando, 1986, p. 23). After long-term anticipation of loss coupled with the exhaustion of long term caregiving and worry, death may not bring pain, but relief that the long ordeal is over. If this is true for the survivors of a single prolonged illness, the potential for a negative outcome for the families of multiple AIDS survivors is unmistakable. A period of mourning following the death of a family member usually allows the bereaved family to accept the reality of the loss, to experience the pain associated with the death, and adjust to life without the deceased. This period allows the mourner to redefine the relationship with the person who lived and died and reinvest one's energy in another relationship (Rando 1986, p. 345). It is acknowledged that the period of intense grief generally subsides in 6 to 12 months, but some symptoms may take more than 3 years to resolve.

The survivors of the first death in the family with HIV/AIDS do not have the luxury of time to heal. Once death from AIDS has become a reality to the survivors, the inevitability of future losses must be faced and anticipatory mourning begins for the remaining survivors. The mother and/or grandmother, sister or aunt will pick up the pieces and continue, knowing they are facing recurrent loss and untimely death. Only when the last of their family's survivors, die will they be able to take time to become whole, and to make a new life for the surviving children and for themselves.

## THE CLINICAL SETTING

The women at risk in the epidemic are disproportionately Hispanic or Black, IV drug users, or sexual partners of IV drug users (Needle, Leach & Graham-Tomasai, 1989). The population that is seen at our facilities, the State University of New York Medical Center at Brooklyn (SUNY) and Kings County Hospital Center (KCHC), has an even larger black component than reflected in the national data because of the large Haitian community in our catchment area. SUNY and KCHC provide more than fourteen HIV- related services, research studies, and education efforts. Some are geared toward women at risk, women of childbearing years and their sexual partners, or women infected with HIV who have not yet developed full blown AIDS. Some provide both inpatient and outpatient medical and psychosocial services to patients with HIV/AIDS. Children are followed through pediatric clinics and pediatric HIV research projects at SUNY and KCHC.

The Infant and Child Learning Center (ICLC), provides an intensive assessment and intervention plan for children with developmental delays and their families. One component of the program is devoted solely to children with HIV infection. In our clinical and research setting, we are directly involved with some of the children and their families enrolled in pediatric AIDS research and/or followed through ICLC. Social support services for families of HIV infected children include practical help such as housing, entitlements, and legal aid and clinical services such as crisis intervention, short term therapy, and bereavement counseling. Weekly support groups help parents and caretakers develop positive coping strategies to deal with the stress and pain that are an integral part of caring for HIV-infected children.

## CAREGIVERS OF CHILDREN PERINATALLY EXPOSED TO HIV

More than any other group of children in need, children who have been infected in utero face the risk of changing caretakers more than once during their short life. The biologic parents of HIV-infected children may be unable to take care of their offspring because of illness, death, or drug use. Maternal drug use seems, in great part, to determine whether a child will live with a biologic parent or not (Caldwell, et al. 1992).

In our clinical setting, we deal with four major groups of caregivers: biologic parents, relatives, foster care mothers, and adoptive parents. There is some interaction between the four groups since a relative may become a legal guardian or a kinship foster mother, and a foster mother may adopt a child she is caring for. Some of the issues are the same for all the caregivers of infected children who have been perinatally exposed to HIV. All have to deal with progressively debilitating illness and the ultimate loss of the child in their care. All have to cope with a stigmatized disease which forces them to secrecy. ICLC offers a program that helps the caregivers disclose the serostatus of their children to schools and day care centers while minimizing the risk of parental disclosure. Disclosure of a child's serostatus and/or a parent's serostatus to HIV-infected children and their siblings are also dealt with when necessary. Some of the issues, however, differ from group to group.

*Biologic parents.* One of the most acute issues faced by biologic parents is to decide whether or not to have a child. At our site, reproductive decisions are often made by women who are not aware of being infected with the human immunodeficiency virus. HIV testing is now offered to every pregnant woman on a voluntary basis. More women are, therefore, discovering early on in their pregnancy that they are HIV-positive. But for many years, mothers often discovered the serostatus of their child only months after the baby's birth, when the infant's failure to thrive and multiple illnesses called for HIV testing. This is also true for the HIV infected women who are unaware of their status and refuse HIV testing during pregnancy. Once pregnant, HIV-infected women may discover their serostatus too late to seek termination or refuse an abortion. Analyzing the practices of women involved in a prospective HIV transmission study at SUNY and KCHC, Sunderland and her colleagues (1992) noted that women refuse to terminate their pregnancy for various reasons, including religious and ethical beliefs about abortion, positive feelings about pregnancy, the fact that the pregnancy was the first with a new partner, and/or psychological inability to make a decision.

Last, there are women who know their serostatus and become pregnant in spite of the risk of infecting their children and further endangering their health as pregnancy compromises their immune system. Drug users may be less likely to use contraception than non-drug users. However, women in both groups will take the chance to become pregnant knowing that 75 to 80% of the children born to HIV-infected mothers will serorevert and not be considered in danger of developing full blown AIDS.

Most of our HIV-infected mothers in Brooklyn live in poverty. They have a history of unsafe sexual practices and many have experimented with drugs. Their life expectancy is dramatically shortened; they face a debilitating and stigmatized illness and an untimely death. Many of them may have experienced losses unrelated to AIDS. If they survive long enough, they have to live through the illness and ultimately the death of their children and, sometimes, their mates. Facing death, they know that their children will be orphans. Denial may be tempting in such an overwhelming situation.

ICLC social workers help the biologic parents avoid denial and plan for future custody of their children. Such planning is made more complex by the fact that one child may be infected and the other not and that children often have different fathers. The stigma of AIDS is so strong that some parents plan for the future of their young children and die without being able to tell their older children and relatives that they have AIDS.

Relatives. According to Michaels and Levine (1992), only 45% of the HIV-infected children who received health care in New York during 1990 lived with a biologic parent, most often a single mother. As AIDS is destroying the younger generation, relatives are called upon to take care of the sick and the children left behind. Even though the biologic parents may still be alive, the grandparents, especially the grandmothers, often become the primary caregivers of their grandchildren. Aunts and uncles, and older siblings may also become surrogate parents. An HIV-infected mother and her children may return to live with her parents or members of her extended family.

Here again the stigma of AIDS makes disclosure particularly difficult. It is not rare that only a few members of the family are told the "family secret". Sometimes only the grandmother is aware of her child's and her grandchild's illness. A grandfather may discover that the grandchild in his care is HIV infected only after his wife and his daughter have died. Older siblings may learn that their mother had AIDS and that their young sibling is infected only after their mother's death. When the parents are dead or unable to care for their children, relatives may choose to become legal guardians or kinship foster parents. They are often advised to become kinship foster parents when they need financial aid to care for the children. However, by doing so, they lose part of their rights as the foster agency becomes the legal guardian of the child and will supervise them.

Foster and adoptive parents. Many children who have been perinatally exposed to HIV do not live with members of their extended family. In 1990, one-third of the HIV-positive children in New York who had been perinatally infected lived with unrelated foster or adoptive parents (Michaels and Levine, 1992). Moreover, these children's caregivers may change many times. Taking care of an HIV-infected child is financially rewarding, and all foster parents are not altruistic. However, many are especially caring and truly involved in the follow-up and upbringing of their foster child. Though the level of adoption is understandably low, several children are adopted by related and unrelated parents who, by doing so, may lose the financial assistance that they would otherwise have received. Some foster mothers have already brought up a family. Some have lost children and relatives to AIDS. Some are themselves HIV-infected. They still find solace in caring for an unrelated, infected child.

## COPING WITH AIDS

Referrals are made for individual and group treatment to help the women infected and/or affected by AIDS. Through our clinical work with them, we are repeatedly struck by the many losses that they have suffered. This becomes evident when following the life of a support group.

The initial purpose of the group was to assist the members with the common themes associated with loss: depression, anxiety, anger, blame, guilt, denial, isolation, "unfinished business." Our goal was to give these women an opportunity to experience anticipatory grief, and to help them create a social support system. At first, group members only sought medical and social information. As they became more comfortable and began trusting each other and the group leaders, they broached more intimate matters. The group began to function as a surrogate family who consoled members at time of loss, attended wakes and funerals, and the group's purpose expanded to include not only anticipatory mourning but also bereavement (Crandles, et al., 1992). As self-disclosure became easier, more women shared their personal histories. Painful memories about their families of origin, their relationships with their parents, siblings and old losses often surfaced.

Arlene, an active and outspoken 49 year-old grandmother who had recently lost a grandchild, recalled the death of her own mother when she was a young girl, and her history of sexual and physical abuse. She spoke of the death of her teenaged son when she was still quite young. Through her tears, she told the group that she did not understand why she was revealing these things since she had never before talked to anybody about these events. The group provided the caring environment that she needed to be able to work through her feelings about her recent loss and to come to terms with her past losses. Barbara, an employed grandmother of 52 who identified strongly with Arlene, later recalled the death of many of her close relatives and grown sons during the civil war in her country and eventually the loss of a talented, beautiful grown daughter who died with AIDS.

The group experienced many casualties. Some members left because they could not bear dealing with the recurring losses in the group and found the desire of other members to discuss their own or their children's prospective deaths intolerable. The majority stayed because they felt that these issues were important and needed to be explored. Some remained in spite of their ambivalence because of the positive feelings experienced and because, in the group, they could feel vulnerable without being threatened.

One natural mother, Cathy, was able to verbalize her ambivalence about coming back to the group after several losses were incurred by members. She worried about what would happen in the coming months and who would be next. In the end, concern for some of the other members and her reluctance to remain home alone made her return to the group. She realized that only in the group was she able to relax and show her vulnerability. The stronger members were able to help both the less motivated parents and those who were immobilized by anger and unresolved mourning. This helped those parents become more active in their surviving children's care, while protecting their own health. Often, with this kind of support and concern, the group members were able to accomplish what individual therapists had been unable to do. This certainly reaffirmed our strong commitment and belief in the purpose of our group. Members developed stronger relationships both within and out of the group setting.

Some HIV-positive mothers admitted that, with the help of the group, they felt better about themselves even though some had lost a child and were ill. They came to realize that there was life after AIDS and that they could be instrumental in making it better. The mixed emotions that these mothers experienced were expressed by Dorothy, a 35-year-old infected mother whose daughter had died with AIDS. She was in the process of taking in a foster care child infected with the virus when she stated, "I feel better about myself than I did before; I am less ashamed and less frightened that others will reject me." Since then, Dorothy has been a strong advocate for education and the resulting change in the behavior and beliefs of women infected with HIV.

The group continued to help members at their time of loss. They would often share their rituals and memories, and reminisce about a particular member or a child's traits with much fondness, tears and laughter. This sharing of the life and death of the child helped to put the death in perspective. Group members helped each other express the sorrow, anger, pain, regrets, guilt, lost dreams and hopes. By confiding in one another they were able to speak of how they missed the dead person and integrate their losses. These experiences promoted a sense of togetherness among the members, and helped them move on with life.

Ella, a tall, attractive, 37-year-old mother, recalled with anger the circumstances following her partner's death. His relatives, who were from a different culture, forced her to wash his body according to their custom. She recalled her anguish, her ambivalent feelings about this event, and her lack of pity for him. Ella expressed the pain and sadness she felt now because she had been unable to properly mourn him. Throughout the many painful experiences recalled in the group, there was time for roaring laughter, fun and mischief that attested to the incredible spirit, sense of humor, and love of life of these women. The group leaders encouraged this heightened appreciation of life that death can bring and urged the members to accomplish what they had put off doing because of their isolation and illness. The therapists often found themselves humbled by the experience and proud to be associated with women for whom they felt so much respect. However, it should also be said that the issues discussed and the decisions made by these women often trigger many ethical dilemmas for the clinical staff that services them. For some, the identification with the patient's situation becomes so strong that the feelings engendered through counter-transference are at times overwhelming and could interfere with treatment unless they are dealt with on a personal level or in a staff support group. Obviously, our experience with an inner-city population in Brooklyn is not representative of the experience of women living with HIV/AIDS throughout the world. However, the issues addressed certainly reflect those faced by the majority of HIV-infected women and their families in the United States. Except in unique and tragic circumstances, relatives and friends experience the final illness and death of a single individual; the period of mourning is limited to recovery from that one death. Not so with this epidemic that sometimes eradicates whole families and frequently leaves parentless siblings. Issues of adjustment, caretaking, anticipatory grief, multiple loss and bereavement impact upon infected women and their families regardless of socio-economic status. Only with adequate support through the illness and bereavement can the survivors heal and face the future with hope.

---

*It is beyond the scope of this paper to discuss the ethics involved in counseling women with HIV regarding making reproductive decisions; the interested reader is referred to an excellent analysis by John D. Arras (1990).*

## REFERENCES

AIDS and reproductive decisions: Having children in fear and trembling. The Milbank Quarterly, p 353-382.

Backer, T. E., Batchelor, W. F., Jones, J.M, & Mays, V. M. Introduction to the Special Issue: Psychology and AIDS. American Psychologist, 43(11), 835-836.

Centers for Disease Control (1992). HIV/AIDS surveillance report, April 1992. Atlanta, GA: US Dept. of Health and Human Services.

Centers for Disease Control (1993). HIV/AIDS surveillance report, February 1993. Atlanta, GA: US Dept. of Health and Human Services.

Crandles, S., Sussman, A., Berthoud, M., Sunderland, A. (1992). Development of a weekly support group for caregivers of children with HIV disease. The AIDS Caregiver,4 (3): 339-351.

Herek, G. M., Glunt E. K. (1988). An epidemic of stigma: Public reactions to AIDS. American Psychologist 43(11):886-891.

Holman, S. (1993). Reproductive decision making in the HIV-positive woman. HIV Clinical Scholars Seminar. State University of New York at Brooklyn.

Kupst, Mary Jo. (1986). Death of a child from a serious illness. In Rando, Therese A. (ed.), Parental loss of a child, Champaign: Research Press, 191-199.

Michaels, D., Levine, C. (1992). Estimates of the number of motherless youth orphaned by AIDS in the United States. JAMA 268(2): 3456-3461.

Needle, R. H., Leach, S., & Graham-Tomasi, R. P. (1989) The human immunodeficiency virus (HIV) epidemic: Epidemiological implications for family professionals. In Macklin, E.D. (Ed.) AIDS and Families. New York: Harrington Park Press, 13-38.

Rando, Therese A. (1986). Death of the adult child. In Rando, T.A. (ed.) Parental Loss of a Child. Champaign: Research Press Company, 221-238.

Rando, Therese A. (1986). The unique issues and impact of the death of a child. In Rando, T.A. (Ed.) Ibid, 5.

Rando, Therese A. (1986). Individual and couples treatment following the death of a child. In Rando, T.A. (Ed.) Ibid, 341-413.

Rando, Therese A. (1986). A comprehensive analysis of anticipatory grief: Perspectives, processes, promises, and problems. In Rando, T.A. (Ed.) Loss and Anticipatory Grief. Lexington: D. C. Heath and Co., 5-43.

Sanders, Catherine M. (1992). How to survive the loss of a child. Rocklin: Prima Publishing.

Tiblier, K. B., Walker, G., Rolland, J. S. (1989). Therapeutic issues when working with families of persons with AIDS. In Macklin, E. D. (Ed.) AIDS and Families. op cit, 81-128.

# THE NURSE AND ACUTE DEATH: DEALING WITH THE THREAT OF DEATH IN THE CARDIAC SURGERY UNIT

Richard S. Blacher and Margaret M. Bedard

As in the oncology ward, the stresses in the Intensive Care Unit often relate to death, but unlike the cancer service, the ICU struggles with what one can call "acute dying," and the strong possibility that it can be warded off. The ICU represents a definition of ambivalence; the patient is there because he is in danger of dying and knows it and therefore would like to be out of it. On the other hand, if he is in danger, what better place can he be than in the ICU? Therefore, he may be very anxious when transferred to the regular hospital floor.

From the nurses' point of view, each patient is in danger of dying. Unlike the oncology nurse who can emotionally distance her/himself from the patient and prepare to lose the patient, the ICU nurse cannot do that -- the very essence of ICU care is the extreme concentration on the recovery of the patient. The nurse must throw herself into the fray with the assumption that all her patients will live if she devotes herself fully to their care. Thus, the ICU nurse is vulnerable to the danger of loss without the usual emotional protection seen in dealing with 'chronic' inexorable dying.

How does the ICU nurse manage to survive emotionally under these circumstances? The implications for the nurses' management of stress go beyond their comfort and even their survival. Anxiety in the nurse may well lead to tension in the patients whose tenuous medical states hardly need the extra burden of the physiological side effects of such anxiety. That the emotional states of the nurses are contagious was dramatically illustrated years ago by Lazarus and Hagens (1968) who demonstrated that when the anxiety of the ICU nurses was addressed, the rate of postcardiotomy psychosis was markedly reduced. All of us working in this area have seen examples of reciprocating anxiety between staff and patient.

The stress of working in a surgical ICU may be reflected in the rapid turnover in personnel from what has been referred to as "burnout." Many units have an average stay of two years. Our Cardiothoracic Unit has a more stable group. Although many nurses leave after a brief stay for both personal and professional reasons, we have a core group with service of up to 10 years, several with over 5 years and even one veteran of 20 years. While this is not unique, the stability of our staff suggests that there are factors in the group which support each individual.

First, of course (and this is a factor of no small import), the death rate following heart surgery has gone down markedly over the past years. This makes the entire enterprise safer emotionally for the medical attendants as well. In earlier years, patients would be treated as if they were delicate pieces of porcelain, and nurses would have to struggle to treat them merely as patients (Lazarus and Hagens, 1968; Blacher, 1972). Yet, deaths do occur, and the nurse must deal with them. A series of techniques are used.

The press of new admissions may give little time for rumination at the time. This has the disadvantage of creating a reservoir of unresolved grief, when a death does occur, which must be confronted in some way. Everyone is supportive. If mistakes have been made, everyone can share memories of similar errors which did not lead to death -- therefore it is demonstrable that it was not the nurse's act alone which was the lethal agent. If the autopsy report can support this, there is much relief for everyone since clearly the other nurses' statements, while possibly true, are at one level seen by all as attempts at support rather than pure candor. If the post-mortem shows an unavoidable cause of death, this reassures everyone that "we did everything we could." This emphasis on "we, the group" by the nursing staff indicates that one useful technique is the sharing of responsibility. The ability to reinvest one's efforts in the care of the next patient is not merely a distraction. More important is its use in reinforcing the sense of self-worth, so important in the type of conscientious person who chooses ICU nursing.

The mechanism of denial may be an absolute necessity in confronting the danger of death on a daily basis. That they are dealing with possible death may be completely ignored by the nurses who can be absolutely stunned by having this pointed out -- at the same time recognizing intellectually that, of course, this is what they refer to as "stress." Another aspect of denial concerns the struggle to see the patient as a person when he is wheeled in, hooked up to numerous monitors, lines and IV medications. To allow his individuality as a person to creep into his/her consciousness is uncomfortable for the beginning nurse. This is brought home when the family gathers around the bedside. It is here that the head nurse may become support for the family until the primary nurse feels comfortable enough to expand her role. Denial of the patient as person, an attitude described so often, may in reality be a survival issue for medical and nursing staffs under certain trying circumstances. The draping of patients in surgery serves another purpose besides providing a sterile field. An eminent surgeon once confided that he felt that he had never operated on a patient's heart. As he walked into the operating room, he "pushed a button" and then was able to repair a "heart-lung preparation." One would never have noticed anything but a concerned, physicianly attitude when observing him at the operating table.

The nurse deals with "patient-as-a-person" in the same way as the physician does by means of emotional titration (Blacher 1979). Drawing closer at times and withdrawing when feelings become too intense, the nurse tries to find a comfortable position in relation to the patient. The head nurse and the support system in general give the nurse, especially the new nurse, the opportunity to back away when she feels the situation is too intense. There is, interestingly, a certain parallel between the nurse in the ICU and a soldier in a combat company. The support provided by a cohesive group of people who trust each other allows the nurse to expose herself to danger with a sense that others will help her if she is in need. Good leadership is obviously a prime requirement for facing danger, and the leader, in this case, the head nurse, needs support systems as well. In our unit this is achieved through weekly rounds with a psychiatric liaison nurse who gives the nurses an opportunity to talk about their feelings in a way that might not be acceptable in general nursing conferences. For example, the nurses are able to talk about not liking certain patients, about their reactions to the medical staff, and the stresses under which they work. The presence of a psychiatrist as a member of the cardiac surgery team allows for immediate discussion of troubling psychological problems of the patients.

The demands on the head nurse are great, and having a competent staff can make her life much easier. She has the opportunity to insure this through the proper selection of replacement nurses. The head nurse must choose applicants who are able to work well with the team of nurses and doctors in the unit -- in other words, the head nurse must judge whether the new applicant can fit in. Candidates must also be able to take on an enormous amount of responsibility. Newcomers are given a very strong orientation period. There is an emphasis on feeling comfortable with the physical setup of the unit. Knowing where emergency equipment is and how to use it, and how to call for medical help or for help in maintaining equipment not only allows the nurse to feel more comfortable but allows her to fit in more easily with the team. It is feeling part of this team that is so important to the nurses' sense of well being. As the nurse shows an ability to work with older crew members, she/he is accepted more and more. This acceptance may be accelerated when newer people become part of the staff and she/he begins to feel a veteran.

An important part of staff morale depends on frequent vacations. Interestingly, newcomers must work for a number of months before they are eligible for any time off. This is a period of great stress since most senior nurses find that going for more than two or three months without some break is too painful. The need to get away from the pressures of intensive care may be really the need to get away from the pressures of of constantly dealing with imminent death.

To recapitulate, the needs of the nursing staff in dealing with the threat of "acute dying" are best met with a strong team approach. This requires 1) a concerned and aware head nurse; 2) the selection by the head nurse of a team that can work well together and with medical colleagues, and is able to take on enormous responsibility; 3) a team supported by the knowledge of techniques and of equipment by trusted team members; 4) the ability to deal emotionally with the problems through discussion groups and with external supports from the medical staff, including a psychiatrist, in the ICU; and 5) strong consideration given to frequent breaks from the pressures by scheduling vacations.

## REFERENCES

Blacher, R.S. 1972. The Hidden Psychosis of Open-Heart Surgery. J American Medical Association, 222:3.

Blacher, R. S. 1979. The Anxiety of the Physician. Man and Medicine, 4:4, 276-278.

Lazarus, H. R. and Hagens, J. R. 1968. Prevention of Psychosis Following Open-Heart Surgery. American Journal of Psychiatry. 124:1190-1195.

# THE GRIEF OF MISCARRIAGE
## Dorothy M. Hai, Ed.D. and Mark S. Tong M.D.

## Introduction

In our society when death occurs, the family mourns and friends sympathize. This response is institutionalized through the funeral. During and after the grieving period, the family and friends continue with life, but everyone acknowledges the loss of a loved one.

But there is one type of death in which this scenario does not occur -- the death of the fetus. To most observers, the fetus has achieved no identity. But to the parents, and especially to the mother, it is a child -- and a miscarriage or spontaneous abortion means the death of that child. Yet there is no funeral; no formal means of giving sympathy. So the parents often feel lost and alone.

Because spontaneous abortions occur in about one-fifth of all pregnancies, it was decided to study the emotional impact of a miscarriage. How did it affect the mother, the father, the parents' relationships with others? This study was designed to examine, in depth, primarily the experiences of the mother and what her grief entails.

## Spontaneous Abortion

Spontaneous abortion is defined as the natural expulsion of a fetus before the 28th week of pregnancy (WHO Report, 1970). We have used the term spontaneous abortion interchangeably with miscarriage, although some dispute exists over the difference, depending on whether the expulsion occurs early or late in the pregnancy.

## Early Research

Most of the work done to date on spontaneous abortion has concerned its physiological etiology and prevention. Javert's classic research (1957) was mainly concerned with clinical aspects, i.e., blighted ova, incompetent cervix, etc. However he did include a section on psychosomatology, where he listed such causes for miscarriages as conflicts in the marriage, negative attitude of the husband, domineering in-laws and fear of pregnancy. Taussig (1936) examined clinical obstetrics to explain the problem. Kavousi (1977) investigated the effect of industrialization on spontaneous abortion rates. Kline, et al. (1977) correlated smoking with higher abortion risk. Petterson (1968) examined biological and social correlates, while James (1974) found predictors for spontaneous abortion in birth order.

The little work that has been done to examine the psychological factors involved in spontaneous abortion tends to deal with causes rather than with effects, e.g., Javert's above-mentioned research. Much of this material analyzes the habitual aborter (three or more spontaneous abortions), such as Hertz's (1973) study where these women were found to have overly-dependent personalities, to develop excess aggressiveness, and to exhibit tendencies toward exaggerated self-control. Likewise, Michel-Wolfrom (1968) showed a correlation between spontaneous abortion and neurosis, unstable marriages and conflicting attitudes towards motherhood; while Kline (1955) found the common characteristic of infantile attachment to the husband and hostility towards the mother. Negative mental health was also shown to be a factor by Mann (1972) and Kalmquist, et al. (1969), who found an association between spontaneous abortion and girlhood bereavement caused by the absence (usually death) of the father.

Few studies or articles have focused on the psychological results of spontaneous abortion, i.e., the grief and loss experienced by the parents. Thullen's (1977) account of the bereavement of stillbirth parents (with a short description of spontaneous aborters) is a classic. He compares the different grief patterns of mother and father, and concludes that one year is the minimum time for sufficient grief. Other works on pregnancy offer brief descriptions of expected grief and loss after miscarriage (Coleman and Coleman, 1977). A recent study in attitudes toward miscarriage indicates that generally people see a need to give emotional support to spontaneous aborters (Hai and Sullivan, 1979).

Recently popular attention has focused on the area of pre-natal and peri-natal death. Coping with a Miscarriage, by Pizer and Palinski, considers mostly the medical aspects of miscarriage, with a few comments on emotional reactions. But their work did not seem to be intended as empirical research, for their results only encompass isolated comments from six women and nine husbands. Motherhood and Mourning, by Peppers and Knapp, is primarily concerned with stillbirth.

Rationale

Since little empirical research has dealt with the psychological aspects of spontaneous abortion, there seemed a need to explore this area in depth, both through looking at the parent's grief, and also by examining the psychological support they received from others.

Earlier work by Hai and Sullivan (1979) indicated a general sensitivity in the population towards miscarriage, but preliminary interviews had revealed a tendency towards withholding the felt sympathy, hence, the term "silent sympathy." In response to this lack of research, and to the phenomenon of silent sympathy, we decided to study emotional support following a spontaneous abortion.

Methodology

Data was gathered through in-depth interviews (30-90 minute) with 24 spontaneous aborters in Western New York. The 24 women were white, lower and middle class, ranging in age from 19 to 40 (median age 29) and in education from 10th grade to high school. Twenty-two were married and most (18, or 75%) had experienced only one miscarriage, while three had two miscarriages and another three had three of them. The total, then, was 33 miscarriages in the group of 24, though many successful pregnancies (birth of a live baby) occurred, with an average of 2.4 successes per subject (the range was 1-6). As part of an on-going study, we are still interviewing women (and husbands), but these 24 participated in the study as a result of either

(a) referrals by local physicians,
(b) response to a newspaper article on the project, or
(c) referrals by other subjects in the study.

Because of the sensitivity of the topic, it would have been virtually impossible to select a random sample. We feel, nonetheless, that these 24 subjects are fairly representative of white, lower and middle class spontaneous aborters.

The interview itself, which was tape-recorded and subsequently transcribed, was based on a questionnaire with 28 items, including demographics, emotional issues (self, husband/partner, children, family, friends, etc.) and emotional support received, as well as questions on the quality of medical care received.

## Results

It was not surprising to us that all 24 of the women experienced sadness and depression -- some quite severely -- after the miscarriage. Even though 61% (14) of the pregnancies had not been planned, and some mothers were even initially unhappy about being pregnant, they still suffered great pain after the loss. A very interesting case was that of Jean, one of the two unmarried subjects. She only knew she was pregnant for one week before the miscarriage (the pregnancy was not planned; in fact, she was on the pill when she conceived), but she broke down in tears several times during the interview. She described a dream she had in the hospital

> I pictured myself in my daughter Tracy's bedroom, and I was holding a baby. It's not my daughter; it's the other one. It feels really warm and nice, and I put the baby down to sleep. Nobody else is in the house and I leave the room for awhile. But when I come back, the baby is not there.

Another woman, Lorraine, who had been very resentful about her pregnancy, also described nightmares she experienced subsequent to her miscarriage:

> I heard a baby cry. I got up, went to the crib, picked the baby up out of the crib to hold it like you do a baby and I looked down and there was nothing

there. I can remember either screaming or crying in my sleep because my husband woke me up and asked me what was wrong.

Other women described feeling "horror, total panic," "devastated," "horrible," "upset and frustrated," after they lost their babies. Even though some seemed to emerge from the depression sooner than others (a few took up to two years to finish the grief process), the initial shock and sense of loss was a common theme with all the subjects.

## Husband's Reaction

Not only did the woman feel upset, but her husband or partner also shared in this loss. Of the 24 subjects, 23 said their partners were distressed (the other did not know his feelings). Rona described the depth of her husband's pain: "He rarely cries. I've seen him cry only three times, and this was one of them."

Lupe's spouse reacted similarly: "He was hurt. He wanted a baby as much as I did. Sometimes he wouldn't talk about it and other times he would. We would get it out and cry a lot and after that we were all right."

Harie's did the same: "He was shocked. It was very rough, let's put it that way. He didn't break down at the hospital, but at home he did."

Even though nearly all the husbands/partners were perceived by the subjects to be upset, five husbands (21%) did not discuss their feelings about the miscarriages with their wives. Betty tried to force her husband to talk about it:

> I really don't know how he feels because he doesn't want to talk about it. One night we got into an argument about it. I said, 'You ought to show your feelings about it. I want to know how you feel.' He said, 'I feel bad, but I try not to think about it.' He's trying to hold it inside; he doesn't want to let it out... He tells me I have to forget about it, but how can I?

However, most of the subjects reported a very supportive relationship with their partners. Carrie said he was, "the only one I could talk with about it besides the woman next door." Some subjects felt they became closer to their partner afterwards, because they began to talk more than they had previously.

The two of the interviewed husbands, Dick and Len, told of their reactions:

> We talked about it a little. But I didn't tell her that I blamed myself for her miscarriage. I probably will later, but right now I don't think she's ready to sit down and talk that seriously about it. She still gets kind of depressed.

When she told me, I went off the deep end, I guess. And I felt rotten. Depressed is what it was. After a while I got over it, then we started talking about it which was a week later, after we settled down. Diana said it was for the best -- the baby could have been deformed -- we both have the same feelings: if it wasn't going to be all right that's the best thing could happen.

Perceived Causes

It is interesting that the theme of, "it is better this way rather than having a deformed baby," emerged frequently. In fact, Lorraine was certain her miscarriage was caused by malformations:

There was something wrong with that baby. I have had two children since then and one has epilepsy and the other has a learning disability. So I feel certain that the first one had problems too.

Verona and Rita had similar feelings:

The one thing that helped me feel better was that the doctors assured me that more than likely if the baby had been born, something would have been wrong with it.

If there was going to be something wrong with the baby, I'm glad that it happened. I don't know how I'd be at handling birth defects that were really serious. That would really throw me or if it would die after birth or during birth.

Even so, 52% (12 of 23) of the subjects blamed themselves, naming everything from overwork, stress, lifting heavy objects, mopping a floor, to traveling as the possible cause:

I went through a time when I kept trying to think of things that could have caused it, like maybe I shouldn't have gone jogging or maybe I had a drink or something like that.

I had taken the pill for five years and then stopped taking it to get pregnant and I got pregnant right away. I can't help but feel the pill had something to do with it.

Emotional Support

It was reassuring that about 83% (20) of the subjects felt they received at least some emotional support. Rita described her experience:

My parents were terrific. My mom is a registered nurse and is into pediatrics and everything, and so she knows what's going on. She was really good. Mom is always there. And my friends were really good about it and they came, but what do you say to somebody, "I heard what happened," or "That's too bad," what do you say? But we talked about it and it was OK. Everybody was there, so I didn't feel as if I was totally by myself. I didn't feel like everybody understood what I felt, but I felt like they tried to understand.

Dee also received help from her mother:

My mother honestly helped me and so did my husband's aunt coming to talk to me, because she'd been through it herself twice. She realized what I was going through and what was coming up. She told me that it would get better and I would feel better, that I might have some tough times ahead, but that eventually the hurt and all that would go away, that eventually you would more or less forget about it, for days anyway. I honestly think that helped me. She just sat right down and just told me that she'd had a miscarriage and she had survived.

Mary's experience was helpful as well:

We were in another county so we weren't in contact with any of our family. They didn't know until after it was over. Our friends were really supportive. I had a lot of people call me and say that the same thing had happened to them or they had several miscarriages and then went on to have children. So we really had a lot of support from other people.

Therefore, most subjects (83%) received some emotional support. However, a large percentage (48%, or 10 out of 21), nearly half our population, expressed a desire for more support than they had. Kathy told her story: "There were different people who, when we went out together, wouldn't mention it. It bothered me, because I guess I didn't want people to think it was just nothing. I wanted them to know it was a loss for us."

Betty wanted her husband's family to acknowledge the miscarriage:

Even if they would just talk to me about it, but they don't. It hurts when they don't say anything about it; they just want to hide it in a closet and I don't feel it should be that way. You need to talk about it to everybody just to get it out.

Doris, too, expressed her frustrations: "My family just thought it was an unimportant miscarriage. They told me, 'Don't worry, you'll get pregnant again.' And when they said that, I felt like I wanted to hit them. I really did. They hadn't gone through it, they didn't know. It was a loss and I felt they should understand it better."

Nadine had problems with co-workers:

> A couple of people I work with made it kind of hard. Recently several of the women at work had miscarriages and some went to the hospital. Fortunately, I didn't have to go the hospital. I went back to work after two days, because I almost felt I had to. One woman at work kept calling me at home and saying, 'your job is waiting for your when you come back.' I thought if she were a real friend, she would tell me not to worry about my work, just to get feeling better. I thought, 'How can you be so unfair and unkind to me? I need some time for emotional as well as physical recovery.'

Some of the subjects, such as Mary, wanted more support from the doctor:

> He really didn't tell me anything. I had to ask everything that I wanted to know. I didn't feel any kind of close relationship with him at all. He was just there; that was about it ... The anesthesiologist, though, was very supportive and talked to me all through the D & C. She was really nice, while my doctor wasn't.

## Previous Perceptions of Subjects

Although all the subjects felt sad and depressed after the spontaneous abortion, 19 of the 24 (or 79%) had never realized such a reaction would occur. Mostly they thought it was something that happens and that's it. Even the six subjects of the nineteen who had known of someone close to them having a spontaneous abortion still did not anticipate the emotional impact. Rita and Kathy had guessed their reactions would be mild: "I just figured I'd handle it. I never thought it would affect me. I'd just forget about; just try again. It's little different after you've gone through it."

One of the subjects, Patricia, was a nurse who used to work the maternity floor in the hospital and had seen many miscarriages. They had still not prepared her for one of her own. "I never put myself in their place and I really didn't know what it was like for them. Now I see what it is."

## Resentment Towards Other Women

For some time after their spontaneous abortions, 38% (9) of the subjects felt resentment towards other women who were pregnant, new or young mothers who did not really want their children, and women who elected induced abortions. Most of the resentment, though, was directed against pregnant women and new mothers. Barbara described her feelings:

When I see little kids or see someone who is pregnant, I wonder if others expressed similar reactions. I felt sorry for myself and thought, 'Oh dear, why me?' It's hard for us to conceive a child anyway and then to have it taken away. I just felt it wasn't fair. I especially had a hard time seeing people who had children close together. Things like that bothered me and people that I thought didn't want their babies but just sort of had them. Then I'd think, 'Gee, why can't it be more even?'

Conclusion

All 24 subjects in this study expressed intense grief and loss after their spontaneous abortions. In addition, 23 of their partners were upset as well (see Table 1), but 21% did not discuss the miscarriage much with the spouse/partner. It was encouraging that 20 of the women felt they had received some emotional support, but about half wished they had been able to get more. And 19 had not realized what the emotional impact of a miscarriage can mean. Finally, 38% (9) of the subjects felt resentment towards pregnant women, new mothers, etc.

This study indicates that support groups are needed, particularly in the first difficult months.

TABLE I
(N=24)

| | Number | Percentage |
|---|---|---|
| Married | 22 | 91.6 |
| Total # spontaneous abortions | 33 | |
| Subjects with one spontaneous abortion | 18 | 75 |
| Average # successful pregnancies | 2.4 | |
| Pregnancies: | | |
|   Planned | 9 of 23* | 39 |
|   Unplanned | 14 of 23 | 61 |
| Subjects felt sad, depressed | 24 | 100 |
| Partner upset | 23 | 95.8 |
| Discussed feelings with partner | 18 of 23 | 79 |
| Subjects received some emotional support | 20 | 83.3 |
| Would have liked more support | 10 of 21 | 47.6 |
| Had not thought about effects of spontaneous abortion | 19 | 79.3 |
| Felt resentment towards other women | 9 | 37.5 |

*Some subjects did not answer all questions.

## REFERENCES

Coleman, Arthur and Libby Coleman. Pregnancy: The Psychological Experience. Des Plains, Illinois: Bantam, 1977.

Hai, Dorothy M. and Deborah Sullivan. "The Silent Sympathy: Attitudes Towards Miscarriage." Presented at the 1979 American Public Health Association Meeting, New York City, November 1979.

Hertz, Dan G. "Rejection of Motherhood: A Psychosomatic Appraisal of Habitual Abortion." Psychosomatics, 14 (4): 241-244, 1973.

James, William H. "Spontaneous Abortion and Birth Order." Journal of Biosocial Science, 6:23-41, 1974.

Javert, Carl T. Spontaneous and Habitual Abortion. New York: McGraw-Hill, 1957.

Kai, L., Halmquist, A., and Nilsson, A. "Psychiatric Aspects of Spontaneous Abortion-II. The Importance of Bereavement, Attachment, and Neurosis in Early Life," Journal of Psychosomatic Research, 13:53-59, 1969.

Kavousi, Nader. "The Effect of Industrialization on Spontaneous Abortion in Iran," Journal of Occupational Medicine, 19(6):419-23, 1977.

Kline, Carl L. "Emotional Illness Associated with Childbirth." American Journal of Obstetrics and Gynecology, (4):748, 1955.

Kline, J., Stein, U.A., Susser, M., Marburton, D. "Smoking: A Risk Factor for Spontaneous Abortion." New England Journal of Medicine, 297(15):793-97, 1977.

Malmquist, A., Kaij, L., and Nilsson, A. "Psychiatric Aspects of Spontaneous Abortion-I. A Matched Control Study of Women with Living Children." Journal of Psychosomatic Research, 13:45-51, 1969.

Mann, Edward C. "Spontaneous Abortions and Miscarriage." in Perspectives in Psychological Obstetrics. New York: Brunner/Mazel, 1972.

Michel-Wolfrom, Helene. "The Psychological Factor in Spontaneous Abortion." Journal of Psychosomatic Research. 12:67-71, 1968.

Peppers, Larry and Knapp, Ronald. Motherhood and Mourning. New York: Praeger Publishers, 1980.

Petterson, Folke. Epidemiology of Early Pregnancy Miscarriage. Upsala University, 1968.

Pizer, Hank and O'Brien Palinski, Christine. Coping with a Miscarriage. New York: Dial Press, 1980.

Spontaneous and Induced Abortion. Technical Report #461. Geneva: World Health Organization, 1970.

Taussig, Frederick. Abortion: Spontaneous and Induced. St. Louis: Mosby, 1936.

Thullen, James D. "When You Can't Cure, Care." Perinatology, November/December 1977, 31-46.

# STAFF REACTIONS TO FETAL DEMISE
## Yvonne M. Parnes

When fetal demise occurs, it is important for staff members to identify their feelings so that professional and personal conflicts may be resolved. When the call came that a favorite patient carrying a primigravida twin gestation had not felt movement for several days, my response was not anxious. I quickly assessed her attitude as she came bouncing in with a friend. She looked well, happy, and still huge! Once she reclined on the table, however, the abdomen appeared less firm, and, on palpation, was mushy. Uterine tone was markedly diminished.

It has become reflex now to reach for the ultrasound scope and hand the second earpiece to the patient. Scanning the abdomen with great patience I felt my own stomach start to knot. I could not pick up one sound. There was that emptiness that now I recognize as a chilling loneliness. I damned the device. It must have been the batteries, I mused. When both fetoscope and an Italian horn one of our doctors uses failed, the patient began to anticipate a problem.

I went out to the doctor with that feeling of disbelief, "knowing," and yet hoping, to be wrong. His response was immediate, and he employed every device, as well as my stethoscope, to no avail. We conferred outside. He was certain. Still hoping, I urged him to allow me to accompany the patient to the hospital and put her on its monitor. His response reflected our mutual sense of impending disaster. He was abrupt -- assuring me that he, "knew how to handle it." Then he complied with my need for confirmation with absolute validity even while looking for hope.

I went back to the patient, who gave me my opening by innocently asking what was wrong. Facing her and taking her hand, I told her that it did not look good. I explained that I was taking her to the hospital for further detection. Her composure was remarkable, but she begged for another of our obstetricians who had evaluated her from the onset of the pregnancy. I put in a call for him and stationed her friend at the hospital entrance to alert him.

On our way to Labor and Delivery, we passed the nurseries. The contrast became so poignant that I felt my mind detach from my body. I was holding and propelling my patient toward confirmation of a negative state, while to the left, was all the beautiful evidence of positive pregnancy pulling at me. I felt like a marionette. Someone was jerking my strings, and not harmoniously.

The speakers of the sensitive hospital monitor were silent. The silence dominated the room. We could hear ourselves breathing, and nothing else. Tragedy quiets suddenly. There is no gentle let-down. It overwhelms like a blanket stifling life. It is painful, while the senses accommodate. You feel helpless. It challenges all the professionalism that has given you stature. You are bare! You must support the patient while coping with a sense of defeat. There are almost no words. The hand you are holding reminds you of what it is necessary to give. You reach out and try. And that is all you can do.

The door burst open and the younger doctor she had asked for took over. He tried again, and then checked the cervix. She had begun to dilate. He became angry. That was his way. He retreated, unreachable for a while. He stimulated recognition in me and I revived to try to support him.

What is it about nursing profession that teaches us to perceive and respond? To read faces of co-workers to a jeopardized patient. Gone are the days when professional demeanor decreed that big girls and boys don't cry. Today we learn to give to each other, as well as to the patient, both emotional and physical ministrations.

Later, in our center, we drew a fibrinogen, took an X-ray, and planned to check the patient daily. In retrospect, I agonized to myself, seeking answers. Of course there are none. How inadequate we feel! How impotent and futile! How lonely and isolated! How unsure and grieving! It was time for soul-searching. I was alone with myself.

Thirty-six hours later, the patient was in labor. We kept her with us, with her husband, friend and mother present until she was almost ready. She was sedated for delivery.

That evening, I went to the hospital to see her. She was on the gynecology floor, away from new mothers and babies. She was composed and quiet. We were aware of each other. There was a sense of finality, but a need to share. Something good was apparent in that night visit. It was more than evidence of caring. We gave to each other. She was not alone.

After discharge the next morning, she remembered that I had asked her to stop in our office. I had wondered if she could go back to that atmosphere of tragedy. She was there! I gave instructions realistically; directions for post-partum care, but without the warm package that usually goes with it. We agreed on frank discussion with her other visitors of what had happened. She and her husband had already begun. I praised her support of us, and asked her to accept some of our support now. I called her frequently, and brought her back earlier than usual for a regular post-partum check.

The last instructions were predicated on hope because she initiated "starting again." We had found no reason not to do so. Next year we will try again. The time will be filled with apprehension, but we will have had a period to reflect on human uncertainty.

Certain occurrences remind us of who we are. We are small and the universe is great. When we think we are super-humans we find we are mere mortals. It is when our sensitivities become obscured, that we must stimulate awareness. We must not allow the defeats to overwhelm us. We must learn from our experiences and become richer. Something is gained when we lose. Even if it is simply sustaining one another, and the patient, this gain can only come from human feeling. And it represents growth!

# GRIEVING WITHOUT GOD
## Marion Cohen

In October 1977, 34 years old and eight months pregnant, I wrote in my diary, "When people say they believe in God, what they're really saying is, 'Hey! Let's pretend there's a God'." Two months later, a typical entry read, "God, please, turn the clock back. Please make me wake up tonight and find I'm still preg and there's still time to induce labor so I don't go overdue. Please-please-please-please. I promise I won't ask any questions." I had decided to pretend that there was a God. For my first personal tragedy had descended: the baby had died. The five stages of grief were attacking me all at once; in particular, I needed someone or something to be angry at and to bargain with.

How, in general does an atheist or an agnostic grieve? Is it harder for her? Would I feel "better" if I believed that Kerin were with God and that the shocking ending to my pregnancy was "God's will." Or if, at least, I believed that our tragedy was "majestic" in some way; that it was important in the scope of world-wide events?

At the time, none of these questions occurred to me: I simply assumed -- and I was probably right -- that nothing could significantly alleviate the nightmare, certainly not believing that God, or anybody, was tending to my baby, when who she wanted and needed was me. Nor could believing that God was keeping her for me, frozen, in a coma, for the moment when I myself died. The thought of waiting three months to begin trying to get pregnant again petrified me; certainly waiting a lifetime would seem phenomenal. God or no-God, I wanted my baby _now_; telling me "even this shall come to pass" or "if Kerin had lived, even this _would have come_ to pass" would certainly provide no comfort. It was the temporary joy for which I was in mourning, and being "deprived" of a God neither increased nor decreased the pain.

Two months to-the-day after the birth, I joined a pregnancy and infant loss support group. There I met mothers who had delivered prematurely, a SIDS couple, one mother whose one-month-old had been killed by a dog, another who, weeks before her stillbirth, had carried around her dead baby. All seemed to share my sentiment: sadness and horror in the present, and not much mention of God or any other hope. There were Jews, Catholics, other agnostics, atheists; no one mentioned heaven, of if anyone did, it was less likely to be a token, and minimal, "But I know she's with Jesus," than an angry, "I know God has reasons but I want to _know_ those reasons." And many who believed their lost children were "with Jesus" were upset by the idea of someone else taking care of them. Once I asked point-blank, "Does God help?" and the answer was, "_Nothing_ helps." There are, I suppose, some people whose faith is so strong, or seems so strong, that it does help, at least on the surface, but these were seldom the emotions I heard expressed.

There are, of course, those believers who "lose faith" after a tragedy, and there are atheists and agnostics who "gain faith" at this time. Allison, for example, a member of my support group who had lost her Megan at 28 weeks' gestation due to *placenta abrupta*, had been brought up to be, and was, an atheist. Her brother, in rebellion, had spent part of his adolescence "flirting" with Catholicism, and Allison had briefly followed suit. Now, about a decade later, the thought of never again seeing Megan was more than she could bear. "I had to grasp at something," she said. "I needed to <u>place</u> Megan somewhere; I needed a <u>place</u> for her."

So she plunged into a frenzied belief in a bad God, an all-powerful being who was holding Megan captive and who would reunite her with her mother provided the latter would believe. She and her husband, also usually an atheist, sought out a pastor for counseling and planned a Christian funeral for Megan.

The actual funeral, however, six weeks after the baby's birth and death, proved to be the beginning of the end of Allison's "faith." "I saw that they <u>loved</u> God," she now says, incredulous." "God is love, they kept saying. And it angered me that anyone who took Megan from me could be described as Love." Another six weeks and Allison was an atheist again.

A year after Megan's birth/death, Allison arranged for the ashes to be removed from the cemetery and brought to their home. This, says Allison, satisfied her need to "place" Megan, at least as well as that desperate plunge into religion. Whether it would have done so in the first weeks she isn't sure; she feels it probably would have. Ten years later, she now says, "The thing that always bothered me was what Megan was missing. So imagining her looking down at us from heaven, and missing everything, was really upsetting to me. Now, that I know she doesn't feel anything, and therefore doesn't know what she's missing, I feel better." In other words, being an atheist again made things easier for Allison.

Meanwhile, as an agnostic, I was not so fortunate. Rather than grasping at God, I grasped at Kerin's photographs, plus the tape-recording and memory of her birth. And I pretty much bore the worse of both worlds -- i.e., horrible corollaries of both God and of no-God. The idea of her looking down and missing us, the idea of her no longer existing at all, the idea of her being happy in heaven and <u>not</u> missing us -- they couldn't <u>all</u> be true; yet I brooded and agonized over them all. And, like Allison, I sometimes had fantasies of a bad God, an *Erlking* type, not so much to place Kerin as to place my own anger and fears. As a poet and writer, I wrote short dialogues between myself and this God -- e.g., the one I mentioned above where I beseeched God to move time backwards. I took for granted that these imagined dialogues and monologues were semi-humorous proofs of the impossibility of God's existence, or at least new insights that would prompt believers to question.

The tragedy rendered me agnostic -- i.e., unknowing -- concerning other ideas as well. Being guilty vs. being powerless -- time going too slowly and me being stuck in the initial acute stages of grief vs. time going too quickly and taking Kerin farther away from me

-- it being the doctors' fault, with all the horrors of "if only" vs. it not being the doctors' fault and thus there being no precautions or reassurances for the next pregnancy -- various contradictory ideas went 'round and 'round in my head, and until I resolved them, I grappled and suffered with them all. What I'm saying is that agnosticism is implicit in the normal, honest grieving process; "healthy, complete" griefwork involves months, sometimes years, of questioning and exploration, emotional if not logical. At least that's been my own experience as well as that of many of the grievers I have known. In our twice-monthly support group meetings, much such exploration has gone on.

Six months into my own loss, when the group discovered that I was writing poetry about my griefwork, it decided to devote one meeting to a reading of this poetry. In introducing my "God-poems," I explained that, although I didn't logically believe in God, I still fantasized, needed, and felt, in this time of stress and powerlessness, the presence of an all-powerful bad God, who for some reason took special delight in harassing "not only me, but certain select individuals." I expected the non-believers to relate well to these poems, and I figured the believers would either be pleasantly tolerant or begin to change their minds.

Instead, this is what happened: Everyone related to them; they laughed and cried. The non-believers probably enjoyed my *reductio ad absurdum*, while the believers probably delighted in being given permission to give vent, at least vicariously, to their anger toward and fear of God. However, by solely observing the reactions to these "God-poems," it was near-impossible to tell the believers from the non-believers.

By 1987 the God-poems had appeared in print many places, and other God-fantasies richly bedeck my pregnancy loss trilogy/journal. Catholics, nuns, and at least one rabbi's wife have read and praised them. What this tells me is that, at least for the type of person who joins support groups or who reads my poetry, atheists and believers grieve in many of the same ways. Neither God nor atheism is much of a comfort in the loss of a loved one, and both types of grievers feel great sorrow, fear, despair and ambivalence.

I didn't intend my writings to be "something for everyone" -- I intended them to be more controversial -- yet it does feel good to know that there is a gut-level which is for everyone. I take care, however, to give the same introduction at readings that I gave at that first support-group. Once, after a reading for the SHARE group in Lancaster, Pa., someone came up to me and said, "It's interesting that you're an agnostic. I'm not sure I believe either, but there's a story about God that I find particularly moving. That story -- do you know it? -- about God and man having walked through the desert together, and you see two sets of footprints all the way except towards the end. `See?' says man to God, `You abandoned me.' `No', answers God, `that's when I was carrying you.' I find that story really moving."

"Yes," I told him, "so do I. But I believe that it's moving, not because that's the way things are, but because that's the way human beings often <u>wish</u> they were. It's the human condition that's moving." He looked thoughtful.

I like to think I am making a difference. But in recent years I have noticed, regrettably, an increase in religious emphasis at support group meetings and conferences, and in bereaved-parent newsletters, and very often I have encountered the patent assumption that a given griever is not only religious but Christian. Roberta Halporn, of the Center for Thanatology Research, speculates that this trend is not surprising, and is due to the increasing popularity of the entire death and dying movement; i.e., it now consists of a greater and therefore more representative cross-section of humanity, thus we find more of the majority types -- those who do believe in a deity.

At the old support group meetings, we used to talk *ad infinitum* about how we got and get "through it," how we keep sane, how we reclaim our lives, and our happiness. Religion was rarely mentioned. What was mentioned were good memories, perhaps ecstatic or especially inspiring or symbolic memories, as well as making something positive come out of our tragedies. Most of us agreed that there is no meaning, God-given or otherwise, to tragedies, certainly no meaning that would make the tragedy worth it. But <u>we</u> can <u>give</u> them meaning -- i.e., make something good happen that wouldn't have otherwise happened. We can discover a better understanding of other bereaved people, and of people in general; make friends we wouldn't have otherwise made; perhaps become more deeply involved in the death-and-dying field as a counselor or caregiver; in the case of pregnancy loss, having or adopting another baby; and sometimes, using one's particular talent in ways one otherwise wouldn't have -- e.g., my own grief-writing and my husband's invention of a new way to use ultrasound. Just as atheists and agnostics find meaning in life, so can we find meaning in death.

---

*I would like to thank my friends Allison Brannigan and Roberta Halporn for helpful, and hopeful discussion. The word "majestic" in the second paragraph is Roberta's.*

# PATIENTS' DISSATISFACTION WITH MEDICAL CARE: THE CASE OF PREGNANCY LOSS
### Judith N. Lasker, Ph.D.

Dissatisfaction with the quality of medical response has been reported by most of the studies of families who suffer the death of an infant during or just after pregnancy. Peppers and Knapp,[1] for instance, in their physicians. Other studies[2,3] have revealed serious complaints either about the physicians or the hospital staff in cases of stillbirth and infant death. In our interviews with thirty-five men and women who had experienced miscarriage, selective abortion, stillbirth, or neonatal death, the same type of results appeared. Of those who commented on their physicians, 64% were dissatisfied, of those who commented on the hospital staff, 40% were dissatisfied in general, and an additional 25% mentioned that although some staff members were wonderful, others were callous or hurtful.

These findings contrast strikingly with the many surveys of patient populations showing a level of satisfaction of 70% or more.[4] Although many people rate the medical system as a whole poorly, they nonetheless are pleased with their own personal physicians. This contradiction suggests that it is important to look at satisfaction not only after routine visits or in surveys of the general population, but also at the time of a crisis, when the behavior of health care professionals takes on the greatest meaning and importance to their patients.

The purpose of this paper is to describe the sources of families' dissatisfaction at the time of the specific crisis of perinatal loss, and to analyze the reasons for it. The rapidly growing trend towards the creation of support groups to fulfill the needs expressed by parents will also be discussed. A better understanding of the reasons for dissatisfaction may indicate ways in which professionals, in cooperation with support groups, may help to alleviate the terrible pain and isolation experienced by these families.

## The Crisis of Reproductive Loss

Each year in the United States, an estimated 900,000 families suffer the loss of an expected child, either through miscarriage (approximately 800,000 per year, or between 15-20% of all recognized conceptions), selective abortions of a deformed fetus, usually after amniocentesis (an unknown but growing number, probably several thousand), stillbirth or neonatal death (each approximately 30,000). Ectopic pregnancies are increasing rapidly and represent a form of reproductive loss as well. It is finally being understood that for many of these families, the loss is a major tragedy, producing the strong emotions ordinarily associated with grief,[5,6] as well as specific feelings of failure, guilt, and despair associated with the inability to produce a healthy child.[1,7] The women involved, as well as their partners, their other children, and related family members, suffer from lack of understanding on the part of the people around them, and develop feelings of isolation, in addition to the grief itself.

## Dissatisfactions with Health Professionals

That patients may be very much satisfied with health services in general, but extremely dissatisfied at the time of a crisis, is demonstrated by the comments of a number of our respondents who were quite happy with their physicians until their tragedies occurred. One woman for instance, said:

> I loved my doctor at first. But when I began to suspect problems, I couldn't even get to speak with him. He wouldn't see me; even called me a nit-picker. My husband and I are both furious with him. All our emotions were basically anger at the doctor.

Another woman reported:

> I had a very fine doctor, highly recommended. But when our baby died, I didn't see the doctor until weeks later. I was very upset and needed to talk to him, so I kept calling and he was just unavailable.

These comments suggest two of the main emerging reasons for anger at both hospital staff and physicians: their failure to be responsive to parents' questions and concerns by providing insufficient information on the causes and consequences of the tragedy, and the failure of doctors and hospital staff to be supportive and understanding of the special needs of families at the time. We will expose each of these aspects separately.

### A. Failure of communication

An important study of patient satisfaction with physicians pointed to the quality of communication as a crucial variable in the evaluation of medical care.[8] Lack of communication is also the key issue for bereaved families, who have many questions, both immediately after the death and again over the following months as they begin to recover. Doyle found, for instance, in a survey of 196 women who had experienced stillbirths, that four-fifths of them were specifically dissatisfied with the information provided by their physicians.[9] The inaccessibility of physicians and their unwillingness to answer questions or to provide information were complaints also voiced by half of the parents interviewed in the present study. For example, one woman whose son was born with a serious defect said:

> A couple of times, when I would say something to the doctor about his condition, he would say, 'Why do you want to know?' Even at the delivery, when I noticed that something was wrong and asked him what it was, he kept saying, 'Nothing... we'll talk about it later' and just gave me sedatives.

Another woman who had miscarried was angry not to have been warned:

> Right before the miscarriage he had examined me and said I was fine. Later he told me he had seen spotting. I wish he had said something and prepared me for what was to happen.

One physician, in commenting on this issue, writes that "Medical personnel generally manage bereavement by treating physical symptoms and prescribing sedatives and avoid discussing feelings...[10] The tendency is to avoid or even reject the grieving family." A study of physicians carried out in England corroborates the impression that many doctor tend to withdraw from patients when an infant dies. Questionnaires were sent to one hundred physicians who had presided at normal births and to one hundred who attended stillbirths, asking about the mother and about the delivery. A significantly greater number of the doctors who attended stillbirths did not return the questionnaires. Those who did were much more likely to leave many questions blank or to respond, "don't know." One even wrote a long letter to explain why he did not have the time to fill in the questionnaire.[11]

What is it that parents want their physicians to respond to? Many deaths carry an element of mystery: Why did it happen? Why now? What could have been done to prevent it? Can it happen again? The death of an infant is never expected or easy to understand, and all of the parents interviewed expressed a strong desire to understand more fully why their baby had died. They sought to make some sense of their experience, to lay to rest their doubts and questions, their fears for future children.

Guilt is an especially strong feeling of parents. Since this baby was a product of their bodies and carried by the woman, they find it hard not to attribute the death to something they did. Both, but specially the mother, examine all of their activities, looking for clues, berating themselves or each other for anything that might be suspect. The following are comments from our interviews: "I blamed myself for everything, trying to figure out what I had done wrong." "I felt my body had betrayed me. It was not working the way it was supposed to." "I kept going over all of the things I did before and during the miscarriage." "Every day I think, why am I being punished; am I such a bad person?"

> I went through a whole guilt thing, wondering if I lifted something. I was to blame, I was inadequate. I produced a demented baby, so I must be demented. It was a reflection of me. This is almost the first assumption you make as a woman.

Many of these doubts could have been alleviated through a full discussion with a physician. Some parents who did express their worries to a doctor were greatly reassured to learn that a specific activity they had greatly worried about was unrelated to their tragedy.

Often several follow-up visits are necessary to explore all of the questions which plague parents during the weeks and months following a miscarriage, stillbirth, or infant death. A detail ignored at first may take on enormous significance later as parents search their memories and as they progress through the many strong emotions of bereavement. Having someone to turn to with their questions allows many parents to make progress in resolving their grief and also gives them a greater sense of control over a chaotic situation where they feel they have lost control.[12] It is not surprising, then, that an unresponsive physician would provoke anger and frustration. Sometimes suspicions about the physician can provoke anger and frustration and questions about the physician's motives. As one woman remarked:

> Every time I asked him a question about the baby's death he got very defensive. I had thought he was my friend, but I began to wonder what he was trying to hide. Finally he said he thought I would feel better if I didn't think about it so much. He couldn't understand that I couldn't help but think about it, and that his answers would have made it easier for me.

### B. Failure of support

Patients generally expect their physicians to be sympathetic and understanding; at a time of crisis, emotional support from health professionals is especially needed and expected. Many bereaved parents spoke of the emotional (and often physical) distancing which they experienced: the physician who never expressed sorrow or even seemed to be blaming the parents, the nurse who claimed it was all for the best, the avoidance of the parents by hospital staff.

Complaints about treatment in hospitals immediately following a birth tragedy were numerous. Most parents mentioned some act that enraged them. For example:

> I was doped up for three days; then when I left the hospital I couldn't cope. It would have been much better if they had not sedated me.

> I arrived at the hospital emergency room knowing the baby had already died and was about to be delivered. The nurse insisted I get out of the car and walk inside because our car was in the way. The baby dropped out on the floor and the nurse gave me a hard time. Then they put me in a room with new mothers -- it was very upsetting.

> The staff was insensitive, callous. They put me on the maternity floor which was very bad. And two days after they had already buried the baby, a nurse came in babbling about arrangements and autopsies. Hospitals just aren't equipped to deal with stillborns.

came in babbling about arrangements and autopsies. Hospitals just aren't equipped to deal with stillborns.

The tendency to adhere strictly to rules or to the needs of hospital efficiency were troubling to many parents. These procedures included the immediate demand for an undertaker or for a decision to let the hospital cremate the baby, the immediate request for autopsy permission, the placement of the mother on a floor or in a room with mothers whose children were well, the refusal to allow fathers to stay with the mothers, or to allow flexible visiting by friends and relatives, and insensitive comments (or failure to make any comment at all). At a time of shock and profound loss, parents saw attempts to console by minimizing the event as cruel. According to one woman who had miscarried:

> The doctor talked to me and tried to say reassuring things like, 'This is nature's way of getting rid of imperfect fetuses; it's really better this way.' Later that helped me to understand what had happened. At first, though, when he said it, it seemed sort of ridiculous, like you should really be happy this happened.

And from a man whose son was stillborn:

> The nurse tried to help by saying it would have been worse if he had died after I had a chance to know him for several years. Sure it would have been worse, but I didn't want him to die now or later. There's always something worse, but that doesn't mean I don't feel miserable right now.

The emphasis on complaints should not obscure the fact that some parents were delighted with their physicians and with the nursing care in the hospital. Forty percent in Pepper's and Knapp's sample, and 35% in our study, either had no complaints or were very grateful to the medical personnel. Some called them "terrific, just like family." That bereaved parents appreciate sympathy is demonstrated by the following comments:

> My doctor was marvelous, incredible. He was our family doctor and a friend, and he never left my beside. He did all the right things.

> The nurses were terrific. They came frequently and talked with me about what happened.

> The doctor was very understanding. When I cried, he put his arm around me. He was very comforting, didn't treat me like an idiot. He acknowledged that I felt bad; didn't tell me not to cry.

In many cases, dissatisfaction focused on one person or event, while other providers were praised.

## Reason for Unsatisfactory Responses

There are several possible explanations for the overwhelming dissatisfaction of parents with some aspect of their medical care.

Physicians, and health care professionals in general, like most people, are uncomfortable around death and tend to avoid both dying patients and bereaved families. It has been suggested, however, that physicians are even more anxious about death than are non-physicians. This behavior may result from self-selection into the medical profession, or from the socializing influence of medical education. Although there has been increased attention to death education in medical schools, the effectiveness of such offerings, which are often short-term electives, has yet to be fully demonstrated. Thullen also point out that "though nurses and physicians receive training on how to care for medical illnesses of their patients, they receive little formal training on how to care for families."[13]

Death represents failure for many health professionals and the death of a fetus or infant is usually so unexpected that it may be considered an even greater failure than most deaths. We use infant mortality rates as a measure of our medical progress as a whole; any contribution to the statistics symbolizes how far we still have to go. Providers may experience a sense of helplessness, and therefore avoid the parents they feel they have failed. They may also suffer from "burnout," as a result of the stress of constantly dealing with high-risk patients. Results of burnout include apathy and even hostility toward the families.

Obstetricians and maternity staff may be more uncomfortable with death than other medical personnel. They are less likely to encounter it, and may even have chosen their fields in order to avoid it. Scully, for example, in her study of obstetrician-gynecologists in residency training, found that some had chosen the field because of the infrequency of death. Other studies suggest that obstetrician-gynecologists are poorly prepared to deal with the dying and have greater difficulty dealing with death than physicians in other specialities. Dickinson and Pearson, in a survey of 1540 physicians, concluded that specialists in obstetrics and gynecology are more likely than other physicians to say that they feel uncomfortable with dying patients and with their families.

The rise of malpractice litigation, particularly in obstetrics in recent years, has made physicians very cautious about their relationships with patients, especially when something goes wrong. Some wonder if they did anything wrong and fear the parents' questions and anger. They often do not understand that anger is a normal part of grief and must be met with understanding. Sometimes their evasiveness increases suspicions on the part of parents.

Many people, including health professionals, do not understand the nature or depth of the parents' grief. They may attempt to minimize the significance of the tragedy: "It could have been worse," "You can always have another baby," they tell parents and themselves. They often do not understand the parent's strong attachment to the expected child, and the need to be with that child, even if deformed or dead, to name and bury and memorialize that child. As one mother of a stillborn child said, "If only I could have held her. Now I have nothing to hold on to. Nothing at all."

Health professionals may be deeply affected by the loss but afraid to show their feelings, to appear "unprofessional." Gilson, for instance, claims that physicians often need to mourn for a dead infant. Nurses and other staff members also may feel overwhelmed at times by their own sense of loss and therefore withdraw from families, who misinterpret the distance as a sign of not caring. As one nurse observed,

> People think the doctors have no feelings. But I've seen them telling parents their baby has died and then a few minutes later find them around the corner or in the staff lounge crying. This affects all of us more than people know.

The following parent's comment confirms this view:

> The doctor told my sister she had felt really sad, but she never said anything to me. In fact, she was very brusque with me. I would have felt so much better if she had been able to share her sadness with me.

All of these explanations are supported by some evidence and offer clues to the behavior of health professionals at the time of a birth tragedy. As yet there have been no studies except Bourne's which survey, in any systematic way, the professional who attended parents experiencing a miscarriage, selective abortion, stillbirth or infant death, and Bourne did not try to explain his findings. A closer understanding of the feelings and perceptions of medical staff may help in preparing them to be better equipped to help parents.

<u>Expansion of Supportive Resources</u>

Fortunately, in the last few years there has been a tremendous increase in understanding the needs of families, resulting both from the research of professionals and from the educational efforts of affected families working through support groups. For example, the work of Kaus and Kennell on maternal infant bonding has exerted significant influence on many newborn nurseries and especially intensive care units; whereas ten years ago, parents were often not allowed to approach their sick or dying babies, they are now actively involved in the baby's care and receive considerable attention and support form the medical staff, including specialized social workers.

Parents who experience stillbirths do not usually stay in the hospital for more than one or two days and until very recently, had rarely benefited from organized programs. In a few places, a nurse or social worker had created a program to seek out and assist the mothers of stillborn babies. Recently attention to these issues has increased dramatically, as is evidenced by a proliferation of conferences, books and articles, and hospital policies designed to help the parents. The recommendations most commonly made include encouraging parents to have time with the baby and to name and bury the baby if they wish, to take a picture to save for the many parents who want it at some later point, to provide other mementos, and to talk with parents about grief both in the hospital and in follow-up visits. Giving the parents choices -- e.g. about autopsy, room assignment (on or off maternity floor) -- supplies some impression of control in a situation in which they may feel they have lost all control.

Parents who have experienced a miscarriage are still the most likely to be ignored, since their contact with the hospital is brief or non-existent, and there is little understanding that, for many, their loss is profoundly felt. However, many parents who have suffered from miscarriage can turn, increasingly, to a support group for help.

Approximately 300 support groups designed specifically for parents who have experienced a loss in pregnancy, now exist throughout the United States. There are also several in Canada and Australia, and at least fifty groups in England. Almost all were created within the last few years. They have been established by parents, by nurses or social workers, and occasionally by physicians or chaplains, and they attempt to reach newly bereaved parents for individual counseling or group support. Many parents can also turn to local chapters of "Compassionate Friends" or other similar groups comprised of parents whose children have died, no matter at what age.

Most organizers report (through personal communication to the author) initial difficulties in obtaining cooperation from physicians and hospitals. Extensive efforts through the media, inservice training with nurses, and sustained contact with hospital personnel have often been required to establish a presence in the hospital, and most importantly, to obtain referrals of bereaved parents. Once established, however, the groups report a tremendous response from families and the rapid development of trained peer counselors, regular meetings, outreach activities, and distribution of literature.

In May, 1983, the first national conference of pregnancy loss support group organizers was held, sponsored by SHARE, a national network of support groups coordinated through the pioneering efforts of Sr. Jane Marie Lamb at St. John's Hospital in Springfield, Illinois. It was attended by 149 people from sixteen states, and was a significant event marking the growth of this new movement.

The rapid growth of support groups to meet the specific needs of families after miscarriage, stillbirth, and infant death is not surprising in light of the dissatisfaction of parents with medical professionals. More important is the need expressed by most parents, no matter how supportive their professional caregivers have been, to talk with people who have been through similar experiences. The recognition of this need, as manifested by the creation of specific organizations, may be attributed to a growing public awareness of the problems surrounding death and bereavement, greater understanding of parent-infant bonding before birth, and the growing numbers of older, prepared, and educated people giving birth.

As research on the subject of infant loss increases, the understanding of medical professionals is bound to grow as well. More support groups will certainly be formed, and fewer parents will complain that their traumatic experience was made worse by the insensitivity of physicians and nurses or by their feelings of isolation. As with many changes in the health care system, these are likely to result from the responsiveness of a few dedicated professionals to the consumers who are directly concerned and who are willing to struggle to make their views known.

## References

1. Peppers, Larry, Knapp, Ronald. Motherhood and Mourning. New York: Praeger Pubs., 1980.

2. Knapp, Ronald, Peppers, Larry. Docotor-Patient Relationships in Fetal/Infant Death Encounters. J of Medical Education 54:775-80, 1979.

3. Di Matteo, MR, Hays R. The Significance of Patients' Perceptions of Physicians' Conduct: A Study of Patient Satisfaction in a Family Practice Center. J Community Health 6:18-35, 1980.

4. Laresen DE, Rootman, I. Physician Role Performance and Patient Satisfaction. Social Science & Medicine 10:29-32, 1976.

5. Pizer, Hank, O'Brien Palinski, Christine. Coping with a Miscarriage. New York: Dial Press, 1980.

6. Turco, R. The Treatment of Unresolved Grief Following Loss of an Infant. Am. J of Obstetrics and Gynecology 141:503-7, 1981.

7. Kline, Car L. Emotional Illness Associated with Childbirth. Am. J. of Obstetrics and Gynecology 4:48, 1955.

8. Todres ID. Communication Between Physician, Patient, and Family in the Pediatric Intensive Care Unit. Critical Care Medicine 21:S383-6, 1993.

9. Doyle, Barbara J. Physician Conduct and Other Factors that Affect Consumer Satisfaction with Medical Care. J of Medical Education 51:793-801, 1967.

10. Chez RA. Acute Grief and Mourning: One Obstetrician's Experience. Obstetrics & Gynecology 85:1059-61, 1995.

11. Gough HG. Doctors' Estimates of the Percentage of Patients whose Problems do not Require Medical Attention. Medical Education 11:380-4, 1979.

12. Shapiro, Johanna, Shapiro, Dean H., Jr. A Preliminary Inquiry into Physician Perceptions of Patient Self-Control. J Medical Education 55:704-08, 1980.

13. Thullen, James D. When You Can't Cure, Care. Perinatology 11:31-46, 1977.

# ANTICIPATORY GRIEF OF THE URBAN SINGLE MOTHER FOR HER MALE CHILD
## LaVone Hazell

The term "anticipatory grief," coined by Dr. Eric Lindemann,[1] refers to grief prior to an actual loss. In many cases, the anticipation syndrome is induced by a diagnosis of terminal illness, such as cancer, AIDS, or sudden traumas which cause comatose states in the patient. As a funeral director, I experience empathic pain each time I stand at a casket with a grieving mother who has lost her male child prematurely to a senseless act of urban violence. It is impossible to count the number of times a single mother said to me, "At least now, I know exactly where he is." Standing on the periphery affords me the unique chance to observe not only a grieving parent, but to see my own reflection as the mother of a male child raised amidst the turbulence of a violent inner city area.

When my son reached puberty, I found it necessary to draw upon a communal support network of extended family, friends, teachers, neighbors, and any other resource that I felt would protect him from the dangers of the street. Enduring endless hours of rap music, noise, and many friends who turned my basement into an after school center and my kitchen into a cafeteria, gave me some reassurance that at least they were all safe. It also gave me a chance to find out any problems brewing in school or in the neighborhood. The network of parents at this time was so strong that a rumor of an impending fight went through the telephone wires like a bolt of lightning and ended with each young man being grounded for the period of time needed to quell the problem. There were never any guarantees, however, that when your child left the house in the morning that he would not be dead by the day's end. What a horrific aura to surround your life; an aura that follows you, not for just a fleeting moment, but remains as close as your shadow.

The leading killer of males, (particularly minorities), aged 15-24 years just in New York City is homicide -- approximately 1,600 males in 1994. In other parts of the nation, such as New Orleans, sixteen year-old males are prearranging their own funerals because they don't expect to reach the age of eighteen. They are under the misguided impression that they are, in some measure, relieving the burden of funeral expenses for the parent, (usually a single female), who is already overwhelmed by the anticipation of their only too possible death. Unfortunately, it is not only the single parent of the young man who has shaped his life around the crime of the streets who grieves the impending death of her child, but even the mother whose child is a hard working citizen or college graduate wears the same cloak of anticipatory grief by virtue of the gender, age and often, the ethnicity which shapes his destiny.

This type of anticipatory grief bears no concrete prognosis affording time to map out a course of treatment with the assistance of professional personnel or to prepare for an inevitable termination. There are no tranquilizing medications that can soothe the pain caused by the death of a healthy young man. No support groups exist for mothers in mourning <u>prior</u> to a homicide. Praying eases the fear, but the tears remain, flowing inside where no one sees.

A mother cannot intellectually justify the homicide of her child by feeling he is out of pain or has suffered enough. She focuses her attention on the life of her child as opposed to his death. Yet, subliminally the anxiety surrounding what may happen, suddenly and without any warning, offers little relief from the gnawing in the pit of her stomach. According to Pine (1974),[2] death occurs at the conclusion of the dying process, and it represents and defines the ultimate loss from which there is no chance to regain what is lost. There is no hope for remission or recovery surrounding a homicide -- just finality.

Metaphorically speaking, a parent should be able to feel that her child is like a bank book, with interest accruing from her sacrifices in time and energy. Unfortunately, even the most dedicated parent in the world may find herself in front of her child's casket, feeling as if the odds of raising a male child to maturity are less than her chances of winning a million dollar lotto prize. The thirteen to twenty-five year investment is suddenly gone, with irreversible results.

On my son's twenty-first birthday, I assisted another funeral director in making a removal of an eighteen year old black male from the Medical Examiners' Office in New York City. There were approximately nine operating tables in the busy M.E.'s morgue. <u>All nine</u> tables were occupied by black males, ranging in age from twelve to twenty-four years. I wondered that evening, as we toasted my son, if I was one of the few fortunate single mothers who at least had earned twenty-one turbulent years of his life by pure luck. I reflected, as I looked at his six foot, slim figure that the cards appeared to be dealt in our favor, but I dare not become too complacent because, according to statistics, I had a minimum of nine years before I could relax.

I asked how the young man that we brought back to the funeral home died. The coroner told us he was shot in a store for stepping on a fifteen year old male's new sneakers. Subsequently, he was left in the store because the police thought he had been robbing the owner. When the ambulance finally arrived, this third year engineering student, home on a spring break from college, was dead.

The irony is that he not only died at the hands of another angry, young black male, but he was condemned because he represents a threat to a society that finds him guilty by genetics. His color was not his fault Rather his particular skin was woven on a pattern formed by his ancestral bloodline, on the measuring tape of time.

There are countless numbers of single mothers who feel the same subliminal pain and helplessness as I do. In spite of the fact that there are other siblings (namely, sisters), living in the same home, the type of worry for a daughter is far less intense than it is for a son.

He is a sitting target, not only for the still discriminatory social practices, but also for the forces of the streets, and the dynamics of parental relationships in his own community.

Within the Afro-American culture, **mothers** raise sons. The Vietnam War, divorce, separation, and family abandonment have depleted the presence of the father in the home. This paternal absence has exacerbated the role of the single mother and has forced her into a very precarious position as a matriarch. Once the backbone of her family, the Afro-American mother must now shoulder the entire responsibility of her offspring, drawing support from her parents, siblings, and friends. It now becomes the burden of the single mother to juggle the dual roles of parent and breadwinner, and to try to find positive male role models for her children.

There are times that I feel so very ashamed, when I walk down the street because I will feel "threatened" by a group of young black men walking toward me. Television and other news media have targeted the young black male as the sole perpetrator of crime. The constant bombardment by the media of these overt and covert messages has placed me and other single mothers in the precarious "catch twenty-two" position of intensely loving our own black male child, yet just as intensely fearing the black male child of someone else.

I felt some relief when my son reached thirteen, again at sixteen, then eighteen, and now on his birthday, at twenty-one. As I looked in his eyes for a very long time, during this night of celebration, I dare not project the sequential stops at twenty-five, twenty-eight and thirty. I dare not.

### References

1. Lindemann, E. Symptomatology and management of acute grief. American Journal of Psychiatry 101, 141-48, 1944.

2. Pine, V. Caretaker of the Dead. New York:Irvington Publishers, 1975.

# THE MYTH OF THE EMPTY NEST
## By Margot Tallmer

Two losses specific to women are popularly supposed to engender suffering in middle-aged women. They are the cessation of the menses (a biological event), and the departure of the children from the home, (a psychological phenomenon). The "empty nest syndrome" has been defined as a depressive reaction to the woman's loss of her children and her maternal functioning. "A connection between her identity as a mother and her ego ideal is disrupted; her self esteem is damaged and the ensuing anger, and her strenuous defensive reactions against this rage, temporarily paralyze efforts to shift to other facets of her valued identity" (Medinger, Varghese, 1981).

Why do negative stereotypes about this period in a woman's life continue to persist, despite all empirical evidence to the contrary? Neither menopause nor the "empty nest," by themselves, are correlated with a decrease in well-being (Kline, C., 1975; Lowenthal et al., 1975; Neugarten, Wood, Kraines and Toomis, 1968). The most obvious explanation is the male belief that a woman's centrality lies in her biological potential; that any aborting of these capabilities inevitably leads to psychic distress. They believe that the inability to further procreate is rendered even more burdensome when the children who do exist do not require constant care. By regarding these phenomenon through such a distorted lens, investigators have been able to disregard the data that clearly shows middle-aged women looking forward to the departure of the children (Lowenthal et al, 1975), that women whose offspring have left have a higher sense of well-being than those living at home with small children (Baruch,G.K., Barnett R.C. 1980), and that "the marriage of the last child is, to a notable extent, negatively associated with emotional distress"(Perlin, 1975). Instead, the claim is made that the depression, fears, and anxiety are not accessible to consciousness in the interview situation.

What a transparent misuse of psychoanalytic concepts! If a phenomenon is not acknowledged but is believed to exist, the belief system is not in error, but rather denial is operating and short-circuiting proof of the belief. Further, the assertion that many adult women manifest at this period of their lives, is perceived as a return to the repressed state rather than as maturational development and evidence of growth. Perhaps the biases of the observer determine the interpretation of the data. Many variables are involved: ethnicity, social class, education, timing and personality variations in the women (certain mothers prefer different life stages; adolescence may be the hardest for some), determine the conclusions of the investigations.

Some ethnic groups such as Cubans and Blacks tend towards extended families, so that the children never truly leave home, but rather rearrange their living quarters. Finally, just as one's ethnic group affects the adjustment to the postparental period, so does social class.

Deutscher (1975), as well as others, found that upper middle class women welcomed freedom which midlife brings from the confinements of housework and child care which they had never found to be satisfying, since health status is correlated with fulfillment.

We would expect that the middle class woman should be in better condition than ever before in history. Good nutrition, vacations, advantages contributing to household help, and other advantages contribute to vigor and stamina.

In recent years, gerontologists working on the life cycle have stressed the timing of life events. Stress supposedly, emanates from the deviation from an expected timing of certain life events (Butler, 1975). In postulating the psychology of the lifespan as a psychology of timing, Neugarten (1968), cites the importance of internalized age norms. Chronological age is not as reliable a marker in middle age because of the wide variety that is possible. Age norms have become much more fluid, but in our culture, we have certain preset expectations of the timing of important life events. The appropriately timed departure of the children is an example of this timing.

There is time to mentally rehearse the departure if the son or daughter leaves to get married in planning and participating this important rite of passage, the wedding. Reactions to being without children are dependent upon the accuracy of our predictions and the quality of life possible after they go. Change qua change is not necessarily unpleasant. It is only if harships must be endured afterwards that change is intrinsically difficult. (For example, a mother who was totally supported by a departed child may need to reorganize her life on a much less rewarding level than before.) Positive attitudes may be engendered by the assumption that marriage of a son or daughter will lead to grandchildren, and the comfort of continuity. Another positive possibility is that issues of identity and autonomy, if only partially resolved in young adulthood, may be resumed, enabling the parent to proceed to even further growth.

The availability of free time for such self examination can be restorative, providing an opportunity for subjective shifts in thinking. A heightened sense of mortality, a common awareness in midlife, is less terrifying when one has dealt with children, and often with the caretaking of older parents. The question, "What will I do when I grow up" has become an existential reality. One can accept the knowledge of being separate and alone, even if closely tied to others, and proceed to develop and grow, or one can retreat to previous islands of safety, endlessly pouring time into grown children, grandchildren, and expanding household responsibilities.

Motherhood is not a unitary phenomenon; it cannot maintain unchanging significance for the woman throughout her life. The burden of being central to family interactions, of experiencing oneself as ever open to interruptions from others who require responsiveness and constant emotional sensitivity, and the inexorable daily tasks demanded by the mere maintenance and mechanics of family life, are all diminished in middle age, and the diminution may be a welcome one. Although continuing, mothering functions on a less intense basis. This diminution may connote a certain loss of power, since the mother plays such an important role in a child's early life, but the gain resides in the consolation that all of one's actions are not so significantly fraught with consequences. One is in greater charge of one's own life

The absence of deep responsibility is not necessarily associated with depression. Children are now in charge of their own lives and the parent is not the sole cause of their behavior. Their departure allows daily life to become much less complicated. The charged presence of adolescents frequently generates a good deal of family tension, and the time right before their departure is often marked by anxiety and internal conflict. Furthermore, many adolescents are sources of competitive envy, blessed as they are by seemingly limitless vigor, attractiveness, and demands for financial and emotional support. To the extent that parents may feel inadequate, the evoked potential for envy rises proportionately, negatively impacting upon family relationships. The departure of children permits the release of massive amounts of energy, and allows narcissism to be rechanneled. Finally, the sexual relationship between the parents is often more satisfactory than ever before. No longer fearful about conception, and uninterrupted by the presence of children, sex may be experienced for the first time as a mutual pleasure, rather than as a solely procreative act.

Difficulties arise when the empty nest is refilled, either by returning children or by ill and aging parents. A middle-aged woman, the mother of three, stated during her session, "I've always watched everybody else growing." She returned to school after her last child had gone off to graduate work. She found herself depressed when a son came home from medical school at the very time of her own final examinations. "I only saw his hungry mouth waiting for me to feed him. I couldn't say, 'I'm glad to see you' when he put his laundry on the kitchen table where I was working. My husband said to put some food on the table, but I told them 'help yourself.' He screamed at me, 'Is that any way to talk to your child?' This is my child who needed me all the time, and was still hungry for milk, still wanting to be the baby."

Another clinical illustration is a recent dream by a woman artist who had abandoned her aspirations for about 25 years and had managed to return to her work. In her dream, she was at the Art Students League. She picked up what she thought was a paint brush, and it turned out to be a bird laying eggs in her hand. (Perhaps the compliant patient somehow knew that the author was preparing a paper on the empty nest!)

As one ages, both men and women are slowly freed from the extended crisis situation of parenthood. Children assume responsibility for their own lives. In middle age, as we have seen, men can examine and reassess their intense, prolonged absorption in work activities, perhaps regretting the neglect of private, personal relationships. They may then decide to concentrate on areas that were slighted, such as affiliation, aesthetics, contemplation.

The male "empty nest" syndrome may then appear. His own dependency needs, previously projected onto his children, must be dealt with. One possible solution is to project them again, this time onto his wife. "I am not dependent, it is she who must be depressed because her children have left, and now she needs me."

Empirically, we witness many men deciding on a divorce after the departure of their children, and then, interestingly enough, beginning another family. Many women, however, permit themselves, at this point in time, the expression of their inhibited so-called masculine, aggressive impulses, now striving for achievement and dominance. They may become more outward in their orientation and may move away from dependence on the husband and the need to emotionally support the family. Some of the child-invested narcissism is then retrieved for personal use, for individual self-expression. To the extent that the husband and family resist the alterations in the woman's orientation, they will attempt to force her back into her previous emotional alliances and priorities. To the extent that she resists their pressure and how effectively she does this, she will determine the extent and fate of her empty nest syndrome. Expressing oneself through others is no longer necessary; in fact, it is frowned upon and denigrated as the concept of a clinging mother. She is faced with a Scylla and Charybdis situation; both solutions are fraught with difficulties and conveniently labelled as female pathology.

We do not have sufficient time to evaluate the other hypotheses that suffering of another up is slighted but one clear example are children's rights and feelings so often neglected. Childhood is presumed to be a Garden of Eden from which no one would want to exit. The facts of childhood depression and suicide are routinely ignored for children do not seem capable of an act of mature self-destruction. Those children must make repeated attempts at suicide to get adult attention paid to their lives. Most do not even mention a child suicide attempt in a support group, not only for defensive reasons, but because of the lack of sophistication about such matter. The recent rash of child abuse cases is reflective of our disregard of the possible problems that children can face.

Society makes the definition of who suffers and how. Platitudes tell us that, for example:

>Artists suffer to create but it is not real suffering.

>Children never want to grow up.

>Old people suffer because they're old and decaying.

Mothers suffer because their children leave them and they have nothing else to do in their lives

Each myth must be carefully scrutinized in regard to the individual for such generalizations cannot be acceptable to every group. Not to have your suffering confirmed when you are in pain or to have others assume you are suffering when you are relatively free of distress, are certainly -- instances of suffering.

## REFERENCES

Barnett, R.C. On the Psychological Well-Being of Women in the Mid Years. New York: Time, Inc. 1980.

Baruch, G.K., Barnett, R.C. If the Study of Midlife had Begun with Women. 1982. Wellesley:Center for Research on Women.

Butler, R.N. Why Survive? Being Old in America 1975. New York:Harper & Row.

Harkins, E.B. "Effects of the Empty Nest Transition on Self-Report of Psychological and Physical Well-Being." J Marriage & Family, 1982. 40:549-56.

Kline, C. "The Socialization Process of Women." The Gerontologist, 1975. 15:486-92.

Lowenthal, M.F., Perlin, P.L. Aging and Mental Disorder in San Francisco: A Social Psychiatric Study. 1975. San Francisco: Jossey-Bass.

Neugarten, B.L., Wood, V., Kraines, R.J., Loomis B. "Womens' Attitudes Toward Menopause" in Neugarten, B.L., ed. Middle Age and Aging: A Reader in Social Psychology. 1968: Chicago: University of Chicago Press, 195-200.

Maddox, G. Eisdorfer C. Some Correlates of Activity and Morale Among the Elderly. 1962. Social Forces 40:254-60.

Medinger, F, Varghese, R. "Psychological Growth and the Impact of Stress in Middle Age." 1981. Int. J of Aging & Human Development. 13:247-63.

Powell, B. "The Empty Nest, Employment, and Psychiatric Symptoms in College-Educated Women." Psychology of Women Qrtly. 1984. 2:35-42.

Spence, D., Lonner T. "The Empty Nest: A Transition within Motherhood." Family Coord. 1981. 20:369-375.

# A FOLLOW-UP OF STUDY OF WIDOWS WHO PARTICIPATED IN A RED CROSS WIDOW'S PROGRAM
### Dorothea R. Hays, Ed.D., R.N.

Samples of 96 subjects who completed a Red Cross Widow's program over 5 years and 40 subjects who dropped out (at a rate of 18%) were interviewed by telephone and mailed questionnaires (72% return rate). Results showed no significant differences in levels of activities on the Kos Activity Index before and after bereavement, nor in relation to years since husband's death, years since attendance in the program, dropping out or completion of program, or type and length of husband's illness. Women with young children had higher activity scores in home child care. Subjects felt they were almost as active now but derived less enjoyment than during husband's lifetime. The Red Cross program was rated helpful by 99% of all who completed and 67% of dropouts. Most of the other subjects experienced too much anxiety and depression among groups of grieving women.

## Purpose of the Study

The overall purposes of this follow-up study were to ascertain the self-perceived activity levels of widows, as related to length and type of husband's illness, time since his death, and participation in a Red Cross Widows' Program.

In addition, descriptive data were sought about the health, work, and dating status of these women and their perceptions of the Red Cross Widow's Program. These purposes are congruent with the mission of PRN, which is to promote research which focuses on factors related to prevention of illness and promotion of health.

## Rationale and Significance

Widows carry a high risk of mental and physical illness during their first year of bereavement (Parkes, 1972). If they perceive their environment as unhelpful, their mental and physical health become worse (Madison, 1968). Shneidman, in his discussion of postvention and survivor victims, stated that "postvention can be viewed as prevention for the next decade or for the next generation." (1973, p.41)

Supportive services, like the Widow-to-Widow Programs, pioneered by Silverman, (1966) are now offered by various religious and sectarian organizations to help widows cope with the stresses of grief and with adjustments to a life without their husbands. The writer has been involved as a volunteer consultant and group leader in one such program.

The First Step Program for Widows was started in 1973 by Helen Miles, R.N., Director of Nursing and Health Programs at the Nassau Chapter of the American Red Cross, and this writer (Miles and Hays, 1975). The program provides a weekly, two-hour discussion group for widows over a period of 3 months, concerning experiences and problems following the death of a husband. The sessions are under the dual leadership of a nurse or social worker and widow, both especially trained for their roles. All leaders volunteer their time. Each group includes 10 to 20 participants. The only charge is a registration fee of $5 for the 3-month period. Two to three new groups are organized each September, January and April. Some groups meet in the evening and others in the afternoon, to accommodate both women who work in the daytime and those who prefer to come during daylight. Routine evaluation of the program consists of a questionnaire administered at the last session asking participants about areas of satisfaction and dissatisfaction with the program and suggestions for changes.

One goal of the program is to give each participant an opportunity to examine her own experiences during the grief period, while at the same time receiving support and reassurances from leaders and members of the group. Another goal is to help members recognize their own inner resources and individual strengths as they plan and rebuild their lives, so that they can again experience satisfaction and fulfillment in their work and leisure time pursuits.

A yearly reunion at a garden party has provided some informal data on the long-term adjustment of participants. Many of the women have maintained friendships with each other that started during the Red Cross Widows' Program, and feel that these friendships have provided continuous support.

Long-term follow-up studies of widows available in the literature deal primarily with the increased risks of morbidity and mortality found during the first year (Glick, 1974; Parkes, 1972), and with changing roles and relationships that often lead to disengagement and isolation (Lopata, 1973). After a comprehensive review of recent research on widows, Hiltz concluded that a need exists for exploring relationships between service programs and social research in the area of widowhood (1978).

The Kos Activity Index (1979) which examines perceived frequency of involvement in various work-related and leisure time activities was used to measure adjustment. Included are 28 items covering four categories:
  (1) social activities,
  (2) work and task related activities,
  (3) productive and recreational activities carried out alone, and
  (4) educational activities.
All activities are rated for frequency of involvement on a Likert-type scale. This instrument was chosen because it is non-threatening to subjects, easy to administer, and provides a new index of adjustment that is not tied to morbidity. For information about validity and reliability see Kos (1979).

Based on the assumption that support systems (such as the Red Cross Program) reduce the stress of bereavement and help the individual to maintain or regain psychological and physical integrity, (Caplan, 1974) and that adjustment takes time, the first six hypotheses were formulated to measure changes in activity levels over time.

HYPOTHESIS #1. Self-perceived activity levels will be lower than before the bereavement for women whose husbands died less than a year ago.

HYPOTHESIS #2. Self-perceived activity levels will be equal to those before the bereavement for women whose husbands died at least a year but less than two years ago.

HYPOTHESIS #3. Self-perceived activity levels will be higher for women whose husbands died two or more years ago than for those whose husbands died less than two years ago.

HYPOTHESIS #4. Self-perceived activity levels will be higher for women who attended the Red Cross First Step Program a year or more ago than for women who attended less than a year ago.

The only systematically collected data on drop-outs from the Red Cross Widow's Program come from the writer's doctoral dissertation (Hays, 1977) which surveyed a sample of 50 participants of the 92 women enrolled in the program between September, 1975 and June, 1976. Nine (18%) of this sample attended from one to three meetings only. Seven of these nine experienced long term illness in their husbands. Reasons for dropping out were not collected systematically. Several of the women mentioned that they felt overwhelmed by the amount of grief present in the group and thought it made them feel worse. They also did not subsequently seek help elsewhere.

These findings indicate that women who drop out of the Red Cross Program may prove to have endured lengthy illnesses with their husbands. Other findings from this dissertation in relation to length of husband's illness indicate that widows whose husbands died suddenly perceived a greater need for emotional support and also received greater support during the first three months of bereavement than women whose husbands were ill for six weeks or longer. This latter group, however, experienced a greater rise of emotional needs throughout the first year than the suddenly bereaved groups, so that by the end of the year both groups experienced equally high needs for emotional supports. Since most supports are offered early in the bereavement, widows whose needs surface only after a delay of three months tend to receive less overall emotional support.

The literature on anticipatory grief is divided regarding its effect on widows. Parkes (1975) found in young widows and widowers greater and more lasting disorganization after sudden death. Silverman (1974), on the other hand, found that widows served by the widow-to-widow program, and who were aware of the terminal nature of the husband's illness, generally did not grieve in advance. The seventh and eighth hypotheses address effects of long term illness.

HYPOTHESIS #6: More of the women whose husband had died suddenly will complete the Red Cross First Step program than those whose husbands died after an extended illness.

HYPOTHESIS #7: Self-perceived activity levels will be higher for women whose husbands died suddenly than for those whose husbands died after extended illness.

Preventive care is particularly important for children. Widows with young children tend to need more support than those without young children (Hays, 1977). Another study of widows noted that most of the subjects with children found the presence of the children helpful because they provided a reason for living. Still, the children were often troublesome and taxed them (Parkes, 1974). The ninth hypothesis deals with this area.

HYPOTHESIS #8: Self-perceived activity levels will be lower for women with children at home under 17 years old, than for women who do not have children under 17 years old at home.

Research findings from a Canadian study (Vachon, Freedman, Formo, Rogers, Lyall and Freeman, 1977) indicate that compared with widows whose husbands died from cardiovascular diseases, a much higher percentage of widows whose husbands died from cancer experienced poor health during the initial bereavement period, and felt worse one to two months after his death than they did immediately afterwards. They were often physically and mentally exhausted from sharing the stresses of their husband's suffering. Two years later, most, but not all, had improved. The last hypothesis deals with the effects of a husband's death from cancer on adjustment after widowhood.

HYPOTHESIS #9: Self-perceived activity levels will be higher for women whose husbands died from causes other than cancer than for those whose husbands died from cancer.

## Methodology

The population from which the study sample was selected from the Program for Widows during the last five years, between January, 1975 and December, 1979. Lists of these participants, including their attendance records, addresses, and phone numbers, were available.

All participants were divided into three categories: (1) Those who completed the program, i.e., attended six or more sessions with at least three attendances occurring during the last half of the twelve-session program, 311 (67%); (2) Those who dropped out, i.e., attended three or fewer sessions, all during the first five sessions of the program, 86 (18%); (3) Those who did not fall into the first two categories, i.e., who attended four or five sessions or whose attendance was irregularly spaced, 68 (15%).

Only the two extreme categories (1) and (2) were used. Samples were chosen from the lists of participants according to the following criteria:

(1) All of the women who dropped out of the program who could be reached by phone and who agreed to participate were included. In all, 40 of the 86 women who had dropped out participated in a telephone interview. Of the 46 women who were not included, 37 had moved away or had changed telephone numbers and could not be traced, 8 could not be reached with three or more phone calls, and one refused to participate.

(2) A random selection of three members from each of the 32 groups who completed the program, who could be reached by phone, and agreed to participate, were included. All subjects who could not be reached or who refused, were replaced, until three subjects per group, or a total of 96 subjects who completed the program were interviewed by telephone. In this process, 56 subjects were eliminated. Twenty-six had moved away or had changed telephone numbers, twenty-four could not be reached with three or more phone calls, two had died, and three refused to participate.

The telephone interviews, which were all conducted by a clinical nurse specialist (the writer), produced ratings of physical health, emotional state, work status, education, dating and remarriage, age of youngest child, if living alone or not, and data to evaluate the First Step Program, including reasons for dropping out and help received from other organizations. All subjects were asked, and agreed to receive, a mailed questionnaire which contained two forms of the Kos Activity Index, to rate activities involved in now and activities involved in before the husband died or became very ill. This type of retrospective pretest design has been found to be more accurate for self-reports than actual pretest/post-test designs. (Howard, 1980)

The questionnaire also required data on the husband's length of illness and whether it was cancer. Sudden death was defined as occurring after illnesses of less than 6 weeks duration. A total of 95 questionnaires out of 136 (72%) were returned in time for statistical analysis. Of these, 92 were included and 3 eliminated because these respondents suffered from chronic illnesses that could affect their activity scores.

118  Women Facing Loss

Pretests and Chi square with significance levels of 0.05 were used to support or reject the 10 hypotheses of this study.

## Findings

The demographic patterns of the 95 subjects were as follows: subjects ranged in age from 37-72 years with a mean of 55 years and a median of 56 years. Their educational level ranged from some high school, 8 (8%), high school graduation, 32 (34%), some college, 31 (32%), college graduation, 11 (12%), to advanced degree, 13 (14%). Their religion was predominantly Jewish: 58 (61%), 24 (25%) were Catholic, 11 (12%) were Protestant, and 2 (2%) gave no religious affiliation.

In order to examine the data in relation to the first four hypotheses, the subjects' activity scores were compared with the number of years that had elapsed since the death of their husbands.

All t values, comparing now and before activities, were scored separately for each of 5 years and combined for 2 years and over since the event of the husband's death marked no significant differences. These findings show an overall stability of perceived activity levels before and after bereavement and for the years that follow.

Since only three subjects were widowed less than one year, there were insufficient data to test hypothesis #1. Hypothesis #2, which predicted no significant difference between present and previous activity scores in the second year, was supported. Hypothesis #3 and #4, which predicted increasing activity scores 2 or more years later, were not supported. A t test comparing now activity scores between all subjects whose husbands died less than 2 years ago ($N$ = 19) with those whose husbands died more than 2 years ago ($N$ = 76) was not significant ($T$ = 0.39).

Hypothesis #5 dealt with time elapsed since attendance at the Red Cross program and activity scores now. The findings showed no significant differences and did not support hypothesis #5, but were in the hypothesized direction.

In order to examine the data in relation to hypothesis #6, activity levels now were compared for subjects who dropped out and for those who completed the Red Cross program. On the basis of a t test, the differences were not significant, but tended in the hypothesized direction. Hypothesis #6 was not supported.

Hypothesis #7 dealt with attendance at the Red Cross program and length of illness of the husband. A Chi square test of .059 showed no significant differences in attendance between subjects whose husbands died suddenly and those husbands were ill 6 weeks or longer. Hypothesis #7 was not supported.

Hypothesis #8 was concerned with now activity levels and length of illness of the husband. A t test comparing the two groups showed no significant differences. Hypothesis #8 was not supported.

Hypothesis #9 dealt with subjects who had young children at home. A t test comparing activity scores of women with children over 17 years showed significantly higher activity level for subjects with young children. These findings were opposite to those hypothesized and did not support hypothesis #9.

The last hypothesis was concerned with the effects of the husband's death from cancer. A t test comparing activity scores now between subjects whose husbands died from cancer with subjects whose husbands died from other causes showed no significant differences. Hypothesis #10 was not supported.

## Discussion of Findings

The activity index did not discriminate between subjects in relation to time since the husband's death, nor since attendance at the Red Cross program, nor in relation to the husband's type or length of illness.

In order to rule out the possibility that increasing age affected the scores and intersected with the time elapsed since the husband's death, activity scores were correlated with the ages of subjects. No significant correlation was shown between age and activity scores now ($r = -0.1578$; $p = 0.063$) and age and activity scores before ($r = 0.056$; $p = 0.296$).

In order to compare the activity index to other indices of adjustment, the subjects' activity scores now were correlated with the subjects' self-reported health and emotional states. A significantly positive correlation showed between ratings of emotional state and activity scores now ($r = 0.2784$; $p = 0.003$); and no correlation between ratings of health and activity scores now ($r = 0.124$; $p = 0.116$).

Several of the subjects who discussed their thoughts about the activity index felt that it was not a good index of their adjustment, because they stayed active even when they felt sad or depressed because they thought it was healthier to be active, or that they might be able to escape for a while from their grief.

The larger difference in standard deviations between activity scores now and before a year after the husband's death coincides with this explanation. Based on data gathered during discussions in the Red Cross program, some women tend to cope with their feelings by increased activity, which is not necessarily enjoyable but keeps them from having difficulty mobilizing themselves. Larger standard deviations occurred also for women who attended the Red Cross program less than a year ago and for subjects who dropped out.

The significantly higher activity scores of mothers with young children merits discussion. Twenty-three mothers comprised this category. The youngest child was 5 years old; 5 mothers had youngest children from 5-9 years old, 12 mothers had youngest children from 10-14 years old and 6 mothers had youngest children from 15-16 years old.

An analysis of the activity sub-scores shows that most of the increased scores were in the area of work-related activities, such as doing housework, gardening, house repairs, and child rearing.

The average age of mothers with young children was 47.6, which is 10 years younger than the mean age of women with older children, 57.7 years. The difference in ages was significant, $t = 6.94$ and may have confounded these findings.

Activity scores were also not affected by attendance in the Red Cross program. Since only 55% of the drop-outs interviewed by telephone returned the activity questionnaires, compared with 81% of the subjects who had completed the Red Cross program, it is possible that this sample of drop-outs is not characteristic of the population of drop-outs. Data from the telephone survey were examined. More than two-thirds of the subjects who found the First Step program helpful, or who attended other programs, returned the questionnaire, while fewer than half did so among subjects who did not find First Step helpful, or who did not attend other programs.

Among the 96 subjects who completed the First Step program, only one (1%) found the group "not helpful," and 4 (4%) found it only, "somewhat helpful." The other 91 (95%) said that the program had helped them.

## Additional Findings

Most of the subjects rated their physical health as excellent, -- 4 (13%) of the subjects whose husbands died from cancer rated their physical health as fair, while only 2 (3%) of the women whose husbands died from other causes rated their health as only fair. Four (10%) of the subjects whose husbands died after long-term illness rated their health as fair compared with 2 (4%) of the suddenly bereaved.

The subjects' rating of emotional state ranged from excellent, 17 (57%); fair, 23 (24%); to poor, 1 (1%). Fair to poor ratings substantially decreased only after the second year had passed.

Fair to poor ratings of emotional state made up 7 (22%) of the subjects whose husbands died of cancer, 17 (27%) of those whose husbands died from other causes, 10 (24%) after long-term illness, and 14 (26%) after sudden death.

Subjects found the opportunity to share their feelings with others who were experiencing the same pain most helpful. They benefitted by talking about their feelings and problems with understanding and caring leaders. They learned how to cope with their problems, found new friends, and felt encouraged to do things. Most (57%) of the 96 women who completed the program stayed in touch with one or more members of their group.

Conclusions and Recommendations

An analysis of the activity scores of 95 widows who participated in a Red Cross program during the last five years showed no significant differences among various subjects grouped by age, length of time since bereavement, attendance, and type and duration of husband's illness. Ratings of poor physical health were more common if the husband died after long-term illness or after cancer, but the numbers who reported such poor health were too small to test for significance. The study identified one important reason for dropping out of the Red Cross program as feeling overwhelmed and depressed in the presence of other grieving women. Methods of quickly identifying bereaved women who tend to react this way and alternative methods of helping them should be sorted out and tested.

Implications for nursing include the need for continued involvement in designing, setting up, and evaluating support programs for widows which foster a healthy adjustment. Mothers of young children should be especially evaluated and offered help with child care and housework.

Recommendations for future research include the development and testing of additional, more sensitive instruments to measure adjustment to bereavement, and to evaluate the outcome of programs designed to help.

Further studies are needed to evaluate the effects of long-term illness of a husband on the health of the surviving widow. Research is also needed to identify such characteristics as help-seeking styles of widows who benefit from a peer group, and characteristics of widows who do not benefit from such an approach.

REFERENCES

Caplan, G. Support systems and community mental health. New York: Behavioral Publications, 1974.

Glick, I.O., Weiss, R., & Parkes, C.M. The first year of bereavement. New York: John Wiley, 1974.

Hays, D. Perceived needs for support of women who participate in a Red Cross widow' program. Unpublished doctoral dissertation, Teacher's College, Columbia University, 1977.

Hiltz, S.R. Widowhood: A roleless role. Marriage and Family Review, 1978 1(6), 1-10.

Howard, G. Response-shift bias, a problem in evaluating interventions with pre/post self-reports. Eval Rev, February, 1980, 4(1), 93-106.

Kos, B. The relationship between valuing of time and self-perceived activity levels in healthy aging individuals. Unpublished doctoral dissertation, Hofstra University, 1979.

Lopata, H.A. Widowhood in an American city. Cambridge: Schenkman, 1973.

Maddison, D. The relevance of conjugal bereavement for preventive psychiatry. Brit J Med Psychol, 1968, 41, 223-233.

Miles, H. & Hays, D. Widowhood. Am J Nursing, February, 1975, 75, 280-282.

Palmore, E. & Luikart, C. Health and social factors related to life satisfaction. In E. Palmore (Ed.), Normal aging II. Durham, NC: Duke University Press, 1974, 180-201.

Parkes, C.M. Determinants of outcome following bereavement. Omega: J Death and Dying, 1975, 6, 303-323.

Parkes, C.M. Bereavement Studies of grief in adult life. New York: John Wiley & Sons, 1972.

Schneidman, E. Deaths of man. New York: Quadrangle, 1973.

Shubin, S. Cancer widows: A special challenge. Nursing '78, April, 1978, 56-60.

Silverman, P. Anticipatory grief from the perspective of widowhood. In B. Schoenberg, et al. (Eds.), Anticipatory grief. New York: Columbia University Press, 1974, 320-330.

Silverman, P. Services for the widowed during the period of bereavement. In: Social Work Practice. New York: Columbia University Press, 1966.

Vachon, M.L.S., Freedman, K., Formo, A., Rogers, J., Lyall, W.A.L., & Freeman, S.J.J. The final illness in cancer: The widow's perspective. Can Med Assoc J, November 19, 1977.

# A PASTORAL VIEW OF WIDOWHOOD
## Carole Smith Torres

In the book of Exodus, Moses makes a statement with which I identify. Responding to God's call, he says; "I have never been eloquent, neither recently nor in the past, nor since you have spoken to your servant; for I am slow of speech and slow of tongue." The text continues, "And the Lord said to him, `Who has made man's mouth? Or, who makes him dumb or deaf or seeing or blind, is it not I, the Lord? Now then go, and I, even I, will be with your mouth, and teach you what you are to say.'" (*Exodus 4:10,11*)

Verbalizing the transitional moods and feelings that overcome the mind, heart, and body when a loss is experienced sometimes defies our best attempts to explain what has occurred. I have experienced loss on numerous occasions during my life. However, whether speaking as a lay individual or as a chaplain, my questions have consistently been answered and my struggles resolved as a result of my faith in God and my appeals for His assistance.

The Apostle Paul said, "My message is not in persuasive words of wisdom, but rather in the demonstration of God's power...." (*I Corinthians*) In the spirit of these words, I feel able to share my own experiences of loss.

I was widowed at the age of thirty-one. Despite anxious moments of feeling incapable of living through the loss, bereavement and the grief, I did survive. I survived because I loved Ralph and could do no other than be a companion for him as he jouneyed toward death and the eternity we believed in. Many memories of that journey will always remain with me.

Because of its very nature, an extended illness inevitably translates into diminished opportunities for social contact and meaningful personal interaction. As the illness intensifies and becomes progressively more debilitating, there exists the possibility that even friends and relatives will subtly put distance between themselves and the patient. However, to assert that this is willful and deliberate or voluntary and defensive or even a combination of these designations is an oversimplified and lopsided assessment. Medical researchers have observed that excessive demands and altered personality traits often accompany other effects in the life of a critically-ill patient as the disease progresses. Even long-standing and intimate marriages have been adversely affected by these phenomena.

For those who are chronically ill, the loss of self-esteem, the impact of unresolved dependency, the erosion of autonomy, and the unsettling feelings of anxiety combine to erode the desire to live. Such patients may attempt to terminate their lives by deliberately refusing to submit to life-saving techniques or by failing to comply with procedures designed to prolong or enhance their prospects for survival.

Caregiving professionals are trained to view the process of death and dying objectively, with compassion, for sure, but also with a proper mix of personal detachment. Yet one never walks away from the battlefield of death undiminished. As death envelops a patient -- whether friend or loved one -- the passing leaves a wound and scars that remain sensitive in memory.

A friend, who is a medical professional had lost her husband to cancer. She wrote to me describing what had happened and what is still present in her life:

> My deepest emotional manifestation of the loss of my 34-year-old husband was a nagging, constant emptiness in the pit of my gut. I thought it would never go away, but found that as time went on, I would find myself caught up in some thought or activity. But as soon as I realized who I was, the reality of the situation returned, along with that feeling in my stomach. My greatest pain came when I tried to imagine what my children were going though and their loss. When I looked at their sometimes smiling faces, I knew they were working their way through anguish because I was trying to do the same thing. You know the old saying, `You have to be strong.' My son, most of all, must have been tormented because his father had always told him that men `don't cry.' My daughter loved her father deeply, and even though almost four years have gone by, I still sense that she is grieving at times. I have remarried, and happily I might say, but I still have times of "sadness."  My son has yet to manifest any resolution to the problem. He seems to be functioning and well adjusted, but I do not believe things are clear in his mind.

I would like to add, from a spiritual point of view, it seemed that God, in His infinite wisdom, build up my spiritual being just prior to my husband's being diagnosed. I have what I consider a very personal relationship with My Lord and Savior Jesus Christ, but at times I clutter the communication lines with self.

God, the Father knows all things and prepares, strengthens and upholds His children, even in the worse times. That is why His children can rejoice, no matter what the situation looks like, because our hope is not in temporal things, but things eternal.

The Apostle Paul gave testimony to support these feelings when He said, "Oh, death, where is thy victory? Oh death, where is thy sting? The sting of death is sin and the power of sin is the law. But thanks be to God , which giveth us the victory through our Lord Jesus Christ." (*I Corinthians*)

# SUICIDE IN THE ELDERLY:
## SOME CRITICAL VARIABLES
Margot Tallmer

The motivation for suicide in the elderly appears relatively simple; that is, considering the many negative psychological, physical and societal factors impinging upon our aging population. Why, then, do we need to speculate further on possible reasons for self destruction? If these factors are so clearly important, why are there not more suicides? Equally intriguing issues for speculation are the disparities in ethnic group rates, socio-economic differences within the suicide group, and the persistent inter-sex variations. For example, men outnumber women in the incidence of successful self-murder at all ages. The aged account for 25% of the reported suicides in the U.S. but at age 65, white men kill themselves at four times the national average, and white females only two times. Here we will concentrate on this phenomenon of gender differences which appears to transcend racial and national boundaries.

Much traditional gerontological literature has stressed the relative ease with which women, *vis á vis* men, are able to cope with growing old, supporting the reasons for the distress men experience. For example, in postulating disengagement theory, Cumming and Henry differentiate the process of aging for each sex. Disengagement is deemed to be an intrinsic, inevitable, irreversible, and self-perpetuating process of aging, characterized by a mutual withdrawal of the older person from his or her society and resulting in higher morale upon completion of the process. The authors distinguished between two major life roles -- the instrumental and the socio-emotional; the former connoting the laboring for a living by the man and the latter, the maintenance of the home and family by the woman.

The female, as these sociologists see her, is permitted, and indeed expected, to continue some portion of her socio-emotional role throughout life while the man's central role of instrumentality will have to be relinquished. Thus retirement from outside work is not seen as a problem for women who do not regard outside work as their major life task, nor require an occupation for status identity or as an index of success. Other writers have gone along with this slightly quaint version of the stability of women's role (Berardo, 1970). However, it has been shown (Tallmer and Kutner, 1969) that disengagement among the aged can be predicted to occur as a concomitant of physical and social insults including physical disability, widowhood or retirement. It is not age, per sé, that brings about disengagement, but the assaults that occur more often to older people. Age alone cannot account for the withdrawal. Disengagement is a clearly not to be equated with suicide but it is possible that the three external factors which affect withdrawal may also have bearing upon self-murder. Further, such assaults may impinge upon men and women differently. We will examine the three stresses to see if they can account for the discrepancies in self-annihilation between men and women.

## GENERAL THEORETICAL CONSIDERATIONS REGARDING SUICIDE

Freud's notion of a death instinct, with suicide then regarded as the turning inward of aggression, has been generally revealed as untenable and unworkable. It certainly does not lend itself to empirical validation.

Menninger's proposal of a three-fold aspect to the suicidal act is also not supported by experimental work: that is, that the act consists of the wish to kill, the wish to be killed and the wish to die. The affective counterparts would be hostility and aggression, guilt and submission, and hopelessness and despair. Again, as in Freudian theory, the internalized love object formerly identified with is killed. However, evidence seems to suggest that older people on a conscious level, are plainly tired of pain, suffering, physical and mental exhaustion, and these factors become more relevant with advancing years. Thus many have minimized the part played by introjected rage, and have instead concentrated on the underlying aspects of depression, notably the negative attitudes of the depressed person towards her or himself, the environment, and the future.

The relationship between depression and suicide is not a clear one. Depression may be an intrinsic component of suicide, the connection may obtain from a common underlying factor, or from an association with a third variable common to both (Kastenbaum, 1975). Disengagement, for example, may mask depression.

## MOTIVATIONAL FACTORS IN SUICIDE

The dependency construct is also considered an important part of theoretical explanations of suicide; that is dependency conflicts (and the opportunities to be dependent) cause many older people to crave retaliation for abandonment, real or fantasized. They may perceive, perhaps accurately, that others wish the older person to die. In some cases, self-death may thus represent a counterphobic measure, a hope for a more meaningful existence in a rebirth phenomenon, or an attempt to save the family. But a call for help is behind the suicide for many people -- seldom altruism.

Clearly suicide is an overdetermined behavior and multiply motivated. Except for the fact that anger and hostility do not quantitatively change a great deal for women until middle age, we do not have too much information concerning male/female differences. Men are alleged to be more aggressive which would account for more self-deaths only if introjected rage and turning of sadism against oneself are highly related to the suicidal act. There are dangers to accepting certain conditions as natural and biologically determined, for society has different prescriptions and nostrums for those who are deemed merely to be fulfilling biological destiny. The results of societal attitudes and actions cannot be dismissed so negligently when we are considering the elderly.

I. Physical factors:

There seems to be little controversy about the many biological advantages of women, but it is nearly impossible to separate out natural physiological endowment and cultural effects, although the issue continues to preoccupy scientists. Some facts seem indisputable; universally, men die at an earlier age than women, and die more often as a result of coronaries and accidents. Infant mortality is greater for males as are intrauterine abortions. There is greater variability among boy babies than girls; that is the X chromosome is more full of genetic material, thus prescribing more behaviors. Conceivably, this increased potential for variation makes boy babies more difficult and irritable, less predictable for the mother, and lays down a model for heightened receptivity to the environment with a lower frustration tolerance.

Acknowledging the potential effects of the sex hormones, Kastenbaum (1972) cites evidence that castration actually shortens the life span of cats. In humans, males are more subject to accidents right after sexual maturation. We have long known of the possibilities for temperament changes in women based on hormonal fluctuations. Pregnant women, for example, have lower suicide rates. Menopause does not appear to precipitate an episode of an affective disorder (Arling, 1976). It is less stressful than believed previously and may be viewed positively. But hormonal effects on both sexes heavily account for mood changes.

If the theories of interjected aggression as a major component of suicide are accepted, males are more aggressive, thus increasing their chances, by definition. Certainly male attempts are often "macho" methods -- guns, explosives, knives. If such lethal methods are utilized, the success rate will be accordingly higher. Women, unaccustomed to strong adventurous, physical solutions, use pills or poisons, perhaps reflecting ambivalence or lack of familiarity with stronger weapons. At any rate, more women attempt suicide than men, and succeed less frequently. As Kastenbaum notes, biology alone is not the answer, as women formerly had as high a rate as men in the United States.

In terms of less pronounced physical differences, cosmetic changes occurring in both sexes are often experienced with a greater negative impact by women. The elderly are a reminder of our own inexorable fate; physical changes in others are threatening. Women seem to be treated with less humanity than men with regard to physical and sexual appearance. Males are described as having strong and powerfully lined faces; character and wisdom their miens. Women are wrinkled, unattractive, and often denoted in terms of negatives -- regrettably, they have lost their looks, and thus, their sexual power. Older women are not subjects for photographs of current social life -- men, such as Picasso or Casals, may be seen on a beach in shorts, their virility (in spite of wrinkles and bulging abdomens) preserved.

Peripherally, it may be noted again in terms of a minor effect, that their perceived lack of strength may assist women as it permits them to live with other people more easily at all points in the life span. Society grants approval to women sharing quarters more readily than it sanctions this for men. Women are also empowered to receive more stroking than males, as well as succorance and nurturance.

Finally, it may be postulated that women may be more resistant to environmental stress. We have noted the greater vulnerability of the male fetus; epidemics have a greater effect on males proportionately, so that this difference may continue throughout life. Sowell (1977) has noted that more men died at Hiroshima and Nagasaki than women and that this pattern of greater resistance is interracial and exists among all males.

II. Work role loss

A. Retirement for men

According to disengagement theorists, retirement is the time when society gives the man license to begin withdrawing. At this point, men suffer from the loss of status conferred upon them and their wives by virtue of their prior occupations, from the lack of suitable role models since other retired men also appear inferior, and lose relationships with former working colleagues. Much of the social life of men is work-related: for example union activities or labor clubs. If a man's job has been prestigious enough he may, in unusual circumstances, continue to confer status on the family after retirement.

The theorists predict some period of maladjustment in retirement for men, although this is generally overcome in a relatively brief time. The strain inherent in this period is largely dependent upon the former occupation. Cumming suggests, in a later article (1964), that if the retired man withdraws from the type of position in which his contribution to society was manifest, he may respond to the commencement of retirement with a sense of loss but subsequently enjoy the satisfaction of having contributed to society's goals. If the results of his efforts could not be seen as helpful to society, he may be temporarily glad to relinquish such a job but later experience difficulties as he lacks symbolic ties with his own past. De Beaver (1972) sees the issue of work which bothers men as the posthumous fate of their career decisions -- others will judge them after death. She further suggests that if a man has engineered events that he regrets, he is traumatized because there is no longer time for reparations. Citing Einstein and the creation of the atomic explosives deemed useful in war time, then later destructively used, she feels he was too old to hope to repair the situation. There was not enough future life left to straighten things out.

Men resolve some of these problems by occasionally reentering the work world, by voluntary instrumental activity, through reducing their ego involvement with the outer environment, reunification with kin, enlistment in certain recreational groups, or by passive mastery leading to enjoyment of the past rather than taking pleasure in what one is today.

Contrary to disengagement theory, the years around retirement are often the most difficult and crucial in a man's life. Clearly voluntary vs. involuntary choice is an important variable as is socio-economic status, the meaning of work, marital status, health goals and potential resources. Retirement seems to affect morale in many subtle but powerful ways; there is a strong relationship between working roles and suicide in older men. Fewer working males commit suicide than retired ones. Work history itself is an important indicator of the possibility of self- murder -- higher rates obtain for those with more disturbed work roles, lower level jobs, and downward job mobility.

We are seeing today the varied effects of early retirement (from 55 years of age and up), and the difficulties faced by angry, middle-aged men who have been "asked" to retire early. One element is that although retirement is an anticipated life event, early retirement can have a powerful negative effect. Mental illness is associated not with retirement itself (Lowenthal, 1967), but with feelings of failure of potential -- a feeling more likely to occur when the work role is aborted precipitously, leaving less time to insure a financial basis for security and means to sustain activity.

B. For Women

1. Mother and Wife

Confusion concerning the psychological effects of the "empty nest" runs rampant. It has been asserted for many years that when the children depart from the home, the consequences are generally negative for the mother, as her prestige is lessened, her centrality in terms of interpersonal relationships eliminated, and her social circle severely diminished. These difficulties occur at a time when the husband is probably still employed full time, so that the wife's role cannot be extended indefinitely. The average age for this to occur for women is 47.

Recent evidence suggests, contrariwise, that middle-aged women in the United States are relatively content and, although often critical of their husbands and the marriage itself, are well able to sustain morale. In fact, middle age is often a time of welcomed lessening of responsibility, renewed attention from the spouse and a closer relationship with him. Money is frequently less of a problem as family numbers diminish. Additionally, adolescents often activate a good deal of family tension as they struggle loudly and unpredictably towards autonomy. Their leavetaking can be an enormous relief to many mothers (Neugarten, et al, 1968), particularly if the children have fared well and merit societal approval. Reflected appraisals may then accrue to the mother. If they have not, there may still be the comfort of not being responsible for all their activities and actions.

The empty nest is an anticipated part of a woman's life. It generally occurs slowly and in stages (child by child, in summer camps, residential schools and the like on a part time basis) so that there can be preparation, rehearsal and planning. Many women are then ready for second careers and a new assessment of life. This comes at an earlier time than a man's retirement (approximately 47 years against 65) so that more options and realistic possibilities exist, for there is more time to acquire new skills, one asks for a job at a younger age, and physical and psychological vigor is generally stronger than at retirement time.

2. Employment outside the home

In much of the research, retirement for men is opposed against widowhood for women as an aging equivalent. The presence of vast numbers of women in the labor market render this comparison absurd. Retirement from the local labor force may constitute, for the female, merely another example of long discrimination and differential treatment, for women not only are affected by retirement but may have experienced many vocational discontinuities throughout the life span (Heyman, 1970). The female labor role is less consistently and clearly defined than the male work role. Women are educated for jobs that they may not pursue until after child-rearing years are complete. This time is, by definition, limited, and then their roles again change. Ultimately, the spouse role disappears for far more women than men and Lopata (1971) has noted that in 70% of widowhood states, the survivor is the wife. Thus, permanence is less often a characteristic of a woman's life than a man's, forcing her to adjust and change behavior throughout the life span -- a good preparation for old age (Kline, 1975) and fitting neatly into a readjustment theory enunciated by Cottrell (1942), and elaborated on by Kline (1975).

We can abandon roles more easily because we have had more numerous rehearsals. Kutner's (1961) theory of the social nature of aging further supports this notion; throughout life we are obliged to adjust to new situations, reach new plateaus, and realign goals, defenses and strategies. Women should excel at this because they have performed the task more frequently. Actually Mulvey (1963) confirms that high satisfaction for women obtains from reentry into a previously abandoned career decision or one that had been put away temporarily, volunteer activities, or a lifetime of splitting working and homemaking. The least happy females had adhered to one job, either homemaking or outside work. Perhaps, mere change *qua* change is satisfying and growth producing. Or it may be that mastery of new skills and roles yields satisfaction. Finally, Dunkle's work (1972) suggests to Kline (1975) that women do indeed throughout their life span undergo more discontinuity and can adjust better to old age. Analysis is needed and questions readily surface. Were the changes voluntary? Did they see the alterations as assisting their husbands and family? What was the meaning of work to these women? Were they holding back on total investment, knowing that change might be necessary? Since the working role for a woman is generally of low status and seldom a top level job, it may be easier to quit (Donahue, et al., 1960).

Finally, Atchley (1976) finds that older women were as work-oriented as men and were apt to need a long period of adjustment to retirement. Clearly, they retire with lower social security benefits, lower pensions, and less chance for re-entry into the labor force. Women are poorer.

III. The Effects of Loss of a Spouse

An oft-repeated explanation of the differential suicide rate in old age has been the greater impact upon the man of the death of a spouse. By the age of 80, one-third of the men and two-thirds of the women are widowed. Both widows and widowers actually have higher death rates and higher psychiatric impairment than married couples: the changes occasioned by the loss are supposedly greater than any other regular phenomenon in the life cycle. Clearly, manifold economic, psychological, and social problems can develop in either sex. That men are the more disadvantaged is based on the following factors.

A. Demographic factors

Women live longer so that more widows exist as a peer group and form the base for a potential system of support. Blau (1961) has strongly related prevalence to the maintenance of morale in old age and to delaying one's conception of self as old. And indeed, after the age of 70, social participation for women may not be diminished by the loss of the husband.

Widowhood for the woman is a fairly predictable event, bearing in mind her longevity and the fact that she is usually younger than her husband. An anticipated phenomenon may be easier to accept especially when one has participated vicariously in the adjustment of other widows. The highest mortality rate among survivors, after one of a couple has died, is for males. They die seven times more frequently (Bernardo, 1970). Emotional distress or the loss of care, of course, renders the organism more vulnerable to infection. Those with similar makeups may marry, a common infection may hurt both, or severe sorrow may occasion the death of the survivor. The question remains, why are males more susceptible to any of these possibilities than females?

B. Roles after widowhood

A major role of the woman as homemaker continues throughout her life. In old age, she is often able to perform this function in the homes of her offspring, thus establishing a place of value for herself in another's home. Women are more likely to live with their children than men and the grandmother role is generally more important and extensive than that of a grandfather. If the husband has been left with children at home, and this is more likely to occur at a younger age, the family organization is disturbed and the widowhood crisis intensified as the man finds difficulty in substituting for his spouse.

In terms of family networks, the wife is likely to have maintained relationships with her own family and these continue as they did before widowhood. Contrariwise, with the men, the kinship interactions diminish nearly as much as if both members of the couple had died. In old age, women are more likely to report psychological symptoms while men complain of changes in social participation (Atchley, 1976). Throughout life, women seem to move along a continuum within roles: that is, they participate to greater or lesser degrees throughout, but actually remain in many of the same roles. For example, women are often daughters in a very real sense until their parents die and are clearly expected by the aging couple to care for and nurture them. Sons are often seen as financial resources, but not responsible for day-to-day support.

Finally, the smaller social network for men may drain the existing relationships as the need for interaction and support increases in old age. But both the widow and the widower can overcome many hazards of old age by becoming involved in a deep network of community relationships and may actually be better off than interdependent married couples without such networks (Bock and Webber, 1970).

C. Psychological Implications

Depending on how deep-rooted the "Archie Bunker" syndrome is, the man may experience difficulties performing "feminine" tasks which have vague and often negative, cultural outlines. Fearful others may depreciate his lowered status implicit in the taking on of the female roles and activities, men are often at a loss for a *modus operandi*. The very activities that can sustain women for indefinite periods, such as housework, knitting, crocheting, and the like, are assumed to be unmanly. It is to be hoped that one fortunate outcome of women's movement will be the extension of these activities into a masculine sphere of acceptance. For many males, however, they trigger an earlier, remembered renunciation of "female" gender identification.

On a less conscious level, males are often dependent upon women for the gratification of many diverse needs, needs often repressed and suppressed. Male nurturant feelings are also forced underground, dispelling as they do, notions of a "machismo" image. The loss of their wives may also deprive them of opportunities to be dependent in a subtle, psychologically manageable form that the two have arrived at throughout a long marriage.

In terms of the bereavement and reaction to the loss of the spouse, women are permitted to grieve more openly and recognize feelings in a helpful, cathartic fashion. They certainly are more likely to consult the mental health professionals than men and to follow the prescribed therapy. And male doctors usually expect a female to be more expressive of emotional problems (Cooperstock, 1971). Of course, the loss of the husband also occurs at an earlier point in the life span, when resources may be at a higher level. The death rate for widows is not far different from the life expectancy of married women; widowers, however, die at a significantly younger rate than married men. The lack of interpersonal support is, of course, great and difficult for both sexes.

Much of this discussion may seem strangely irrelevant to the many widows who often cannot participate fully in the life of the society. They are woefully poor and tragically discriminated against financially, victimized often. Figures vary throughout the country and according to different reports, but none deny the financial inequities; in 1988, about one half of people over 65 had less than $1,350 a year, and these were mostly females. The social security system discriminates against them so that women not only retire on lower pensions but receive unfairly, far lower benefits.

Many women are members of minority groups, or foreign-born and have been less exposed than their husbands to the management of their finances, and dealing with urban bureaucracies to obtain the type of social services to which they are entitled. Yet even among these groups, with severely limited economic resources, the male/female ration of suicide tilts toward a predominance of males.

It is clear that a mythology of gender difference prevails among the majority of social science researchers based on prejudiced readings of the data that do exist. If we are ever going to really diagnose the causes of suicide among the elderly, much more clear-sighted study remains to be done.

## REFERENCES

Arling, G. "Resistance to Isolation Among Elderly Widows." Int.J of Aging & Human Development. 1976 7(1) 67-80.

Atchley, R.C. "Selected Social and Psychological Differences Between Men and Women in Later Life." J of Gerontology, 1976 Vol. 31:2, pp. 204-211.

Berardo F. "Survivorship and Social Isolation: the Case of the Aged Widower." The Family Coordinator 19 January 1970, pp. 11-25.

Blau, Z.S. "Structural Constraints on Friendship in Old Age." American Sociological Review.1961, 26 (3), pp. 429-439.

Bock, E. W, Webber, I.H. "Marriage and Suicide: Reinforcing and Alternative Relationships for Elderly Males." Paper presented at the Annual Meeting of the National Conference on Family Relations. October 1970.

Bock, E.W., Webber, IL. "Suicide among the Elderly: Isolating Widowhood and Mitigating Alternatives." J of Marriage and the Family, February 1972, pp. 24-30.

Cantor, M. "Older Women and Income Adequacy." Paper presented at a Symposium on the Problems of the Elderly in New York City: A Crisis for the Elderly Woman, February 25, 1976.

Clark, N.,Anderson, B. Culture and Aging. Springfield: Charles C. Thomas, 1967.

Cooperstock, R. "Sex Differences in the Use of Mood-Modifying Drugs: An Explanatory Model." J of Health and Social Behavior. February 1971, 12. pp. 230-244.

Cottrell, L.S. Jr. "The Adjustment of the Individual to his Age and Sex Roles." American Sociological Review, 1942, 7.

Cumming, E. New Thoughts on the Theory of Disengagement." In Kastenbaum, R. (Ed.), New Thoughts on Old Age. New York: Springer, 1964, Chapter 1.

de Beaver S. Coming of Age New York: G.P. Putnam Sons, 1972.

Donahue, W., Orbach, H., and Pollack, 0. "Retirement: The Emerging Social Pattern." In C. Tibbits, ed., Handbook of Social Gerontology. Chicago: University of Chicago Press, 1960.

Dunkel, R.E., "Life Experiences of Women and Old Age." Paper presented at the 25th Annual Meeting of the Gerontological Society, San Juan, December 17-21, 1972.

Heyman,D.K. "Does a Wife Retire?" The Gerontologist, 1970:10. 54-60.

Heyman, D.K., Jeffers, F.C."Wives and Retirement: A Pilot Study." J of Gerontology, 1968:23, pp. 488-496.

Kastenbaum, R. The Psychology of Death. 1972. New York: Springer Pubs.

Kline, C."The Socialization Process of Women." The Gerontologist 1975. 15 (6), pp. 486-492.

Kutner, B. "The Social Nature of Aging." Paper presented at the American Psychological Association, New York City, 1961.

Lopata, H.Z. "Widows as a Minority Group." Gerontologist, Spring 1971, Part II, pp. 67-77.

Lowenthal, M.F., Berkman, P.L. Aging and Mental Disorder in San Francisco: A Social Psychiatric Study. San Francisco: Jossey-Bass, 1967.

Neugarten, B.L., Wood, V., Kraines, R.J., Loomis, B. Women's Attitudes toward the Menopause," in B.L. Neugarten (ed.), Middle Age and Aging: A Reader in Social Psychology. Chicago: University of Chicago Press, 1968, pp. 195-200.

Resnick, H.L., Cantor,J. "Suicide and Aging." J of American Geriatric Society, Vol. XVIII, 1970, pp. 152-158.

Sowell, T. "Black-White I.Q. Controversy." New York Times Magazine, March 27, 1977, pp. 57-62.

Streib, G.F., Schneider, C.J. Retirement in American Society, Ithaca: Cornell University Press, 1971.

Tallmer, M., Kutner, B. "Disengagement and the Stresses of Aging." J of Gerontology 1969: 24, pp. 70-75.

Walsh, D., McCarthy, P.D. "Suicide in Dublin's Elderly." 1981.

Winokur, G. "Depression in the Menopause." American J of Psychiatry 130:1, January 1973, pp. 92-93.

## CONTRIBUTORS

Henry Berger, M.D. is a professor at the New York Hospital-Cornell Medical Center, New York, N.Y.

Richard S. Blacher, M.D. is a Professor of Psychiatry and Lecturer in Surgery, Tufts-New England Medical Center, Boston, MA.

Chantal Bruchez-Hall, Ph.D., is a Clinical Assistant Professor, Department of Psychiatry, at State University of New York-Health Science Center at Brooklyn.

Marion Cohen, Ph.D., holds a Doctorate in mathematics and is the published author of over twelve works of poetry dealing with loss.

Meeta Goswami, Ph.D., MPH is Director of the Narcolepsy Institute, Sleep-Wake Disorders Center, Montefiore Medical Center, Albert Einstein College of Medicien, Bronx, N.Y.

Elizabeth J. Clark, Ph.D.,M.S.W., Department of Social Work, Albany Medical Center, Albany, N.Y.

Dr. Steven Gullo, Ph.D. is President, Institute for Health and Weight Sciences, Center for Healthful Living; Director of Health Planning and Services, American Institute of Life-Threatening Illness and Loss, New York, N.Y.

Roberta Halporn, M.A., is Director of the Center for Thanatology Research and Education, Inc., Brooklyn, N.Y., and Publishing Liaison for the American Institute of Life-Threatening Illness and Loss.

LaVone Hazell, M.S., is a certified Family Therapist from Fordham University, and is manager of the Marcus Jackson Funeral Home in New York City.

Rose Savage Jackman is an advocate for breast health and a breast cancer survivor. She is also a graduate student in Public Health at Hunter College, School of Health Science.

Austin H. Kutscher, is Professor-Emeritus, Department of Psychiatry in Dentistry, Psychiatric Institute, Columbia University College of Physicians & Surgeons, New York, N.Y.; President of the American Institute of Life Threatening Illness and Loss.

Nanette Nelson, Ph.D., is a Clinical Assistant Professor, Department of Psychiatry, State University of New York-Health Science Center at Brooklyn, N. Y.

Irene Seeland, M.D., Formerly Assistant Clinical Professor of Psychiatry, New York Medical Center, Attending Psychiatrist, Goldwater Memorial Hospital, New York, N.Y.

Florence E. Selder, Ph.D., R.N. is Associate Professor and Urban Research Center Scientist, University of Wisconsin, Milwaukee, WI.

Mary-Ellen Siegel, M.S.W., A.C.S.W., Senior Teaching Associate, Department of Community Medicine, Mt. Sinai School of Medicine, New York, N.Y.

Chaplain Carole Smith-Torres was formerly Pastoral Associate, the Presbyterian Hospital in the City of New York, Conservative Baptist Mission Society, Staten Island, N.Y.

Anita Sussman, CSW-MSW, is Coordinator and Supervisor of the Infant and Child Learning Center, State University of New York-Health Science Center, Brooklyn, New York.

Margot Tallmer, Ph.D. is Professor at the Brookdale Center on Aging, Hunter College of City University of N.Y., New York, N.Y.

Richard Torpie, M.D. is Associate in Radiology, Department of Radiology, St. Luke's Hospital, Bethlehem, PA.

## YOU MAY ALSO BE INTERESTED IN:

CHEMOTHERAPY AND CANCER: Care of the Patient, Family & Staff.
Robert DeBellis, M.D., Oncologist, Columbia Physicians & Surgeons, Irene B. Seeland, A.H. Kutscher and Florence Selder, Editors
1992  120pp.  Paper $15.95

●

PERSPECTIVES ON THE AIDS CRISIS: THANATOLOGIC ASPECTS
Dr. Robert S. Lamke, M.D., Attending Psychiatrist, Kings County Hospital, Marcia Fishman, Dr. Austin H. Kutscher, Dr. Carlo E. Grossi, M.D., Editors
1989  140 pp.  Paper $15.95

●

THE PEDIATRIC NURSE & LIFE-THREATENED CHILD
Penelope Buschman, Nursing Associate, Babies Hospital, New York, John Schowalter & Austin H. Kutscher, Editors
1986 100pp.  Paper $14.95

*Whether a professional from another discipline or a parent ... of a very ill child, this volume is a resource. The children's care subspecialty is a tough one and the help here will be welcome.*
American Journal of Hospice Care

●

MUSCULAR DYSTROPHY AND ALLIED DISEASES: Impact on Patients, Family, and Staff
Leon I. Charash, Chair, Medical Advisory Committee, MD Association, Arlene Bregman, Elisabeth P. Prichard, et al. Editors
1988  90pp.  Paper $13.95

●

BEYOND LOSS. A Practical Guide Through Grief to a Meaningful Life
Lilly Singer, Margaret Sirot, and Susan Rodd.
*A long-needed and welcome addition to the field. ...both pragmatic and compassionate. ...*
Rabbi Earl Grollman
1988  162 pp.  Cloth $15.95

●

HELPING EACH OTHER IN WIDOWHOOD, Phyllis Silverman, Ph.D., Harvard Medical School, et al.
Initiating Widow-to Widow groups, by the pioneer who established them.
1975  212 pp.  Cloth $8.95

IF YOU WILL LIFT THE LOAD: A GUIDE TO FORMING WIDOWHOOD GROUPS. By Dr. Silverman, et al.
●  Pap. $8.95

---

(All texts are available from standard jobbers as well as direct)

The Center for Thanatology Research, 391 Atlantic Ave., Brooklyn, N.Y. 11217-1701
Write for our Free Catalog